HESIOD AND THE NEAR EAST

HESIOD
AND THE
NEAR EAST

By

P. WALCOT

CARDIFF
UNIVERSITY OF WALES PRESS
1966

PRINTED IN GREAT BRITAIN
BY WILLIAM LEWIS (PRINTERS) LTD., CARDIFF

ACKNOWLEDGEMENTS

My interest in Hesiod has gained me many friends throughout the world, and to all of these, in Europe, in North America, and in Australia, I wish to express my gratitude. I am especially indebted to the three friends who read the draft of this book and laboured hard to improve its phrasing and its contents, Professors B. R. Rees, L. J. D. Richardson, and T. B. L. Webster. Without Professor Rees' unfailing support and encouragement my work would never have been completed; Professor Richardson, however busy, always found time to discuss my current problem; in my first term as an undergraduate at University College London – and now, like Hesiod, I turn for a moment to autobiography – I attended Professor Webster's lectures on the Works and Days, and such was the impression which they created that, when several years later I was invited to conduct research, I chose to study the poet from Ascra. I must also thank W. G. Lambert, on whose time, patience, and erudition I drew heavily. In particular I am grateful to him for reading the draft of chapter two and for allowing me to use material being prepared for publication. The imperfections which remain and the views advanced in the book are, of course, solely my own responsibility.

The grant of a Leverhulme Research Award gave me access to libraries in London and elsewhere, and I close this 'catalogue' of acknowledgements by thanking the Leverhulme Trustees for their generosity.

P.W.

July 1965.

CONTENTS

ABBREVIATIONS

Abbreviations adopted in referring to books are as follows:

ANET . J. B. Pritchard (ed.), *Ancient Near Eastern Texts relating to the Old Testament* (Princeton², 1955).

Driver . . G. R. Driver, *Canaanite Myths and Legends* (Old Testament Studies 3, Edinburgh, 1956).

Éléments . O. Eissfeldt and others, *Éléments orientaux dans la Religion grecque ancienne* (Paris, 1960).

Mythologies . S. N. Kramer (ed.), *Mythologies of the Ancient World* (Garden City, New York, 1961).

Naissance . S. Sauneron and others, *La Naissance du Monde* (Sources Orientales 1, Paris, 1959).

Sagesses . . J. Leclant and others, *Les Sagesses du Proche-Orient ancien* (Paris, 1963).

For periodicals I have used the abbreviations to be found in *L'Année Philologique*, but with the following exceptions:

JCS . . *Journal of Cuneiform Studies.*
JNES . . *Journal of Near Eastern Studies.*
RAA . . *Revue d'Assyriologie et d'Archéologie orientale.*

INTRODUCTION

UNTIL recently, if one wished to attempt a comparative study of Hesiod, all one had of early date was the poetry of Homer. The last twenty years, however, have made us increasingly aware of the existence in the Near East of a whole range of literature, including creation myths and didactic treatises, infinitely older than any Greek text which we possess. Nobody can aspire to mastery of all the languages in which our texts from Asia Minor, from the Levant, from Mesopotamia, and from Egypt are written, but we have been well served by specialists in each particular language, so that we may today consult with confidence standard collections of texts in translation.[1] In this book I propose to examine a considerable number of Near Eastern texts and to discuss their relationship to Hesiod's Theogony and Works and Days. Others before me have studied the Near Eastern background of Hesiod's poems, especially in the case of the Theogony. I have no desire to denigrate their efforts, for it is my belief that what has been said of Julian the Apostate, that he was 'intolerant of any nonsense that was not his own', describes almost anybody who writes on the subject of early Greek poetry. But if I were pressed for a candid opinion, I would state that, while I owe them much, scholars who have previously examined Hesiod and the influence of the Near East have been over-hasty. They have snatched at the Hittite Kumarbi myth, and, ignoring the facts that its links with the Theogony are not so very numerous and close, and that this text is not even Hittite in origin, have neglected the equally important clues offered by Babylonian literature. A handful of scholars provides a noteworthy exception, but their impact appears to have been slight and few look far beyond the borders of Anatolia. Egypt has fared much worse, although I hope to show that it also is relevant to a study of the Theogony. Already it might be felt that I am being perverse in trying to complicate something which before seemed straightforward and direct. This, however, is precisely what has been wrong with other attempts to establish the relationship between Hesiod and the Near East: the picture has been far too simple, so simple in fact that one immediately becomes suspicious. It is convenient to believe that the Hittite Kumarbi and Ullikummi myths influenced the Theogony and that the residence of Hesiod's father at Cyme in Aeolis provided the point of contact between Greek and Hittite traditions. Here we have the complete problem of influence and transmission solved in a single sentence. Yet I doubt whether the truth can ever be expressed quite as concisely as this, and my own effort to answer the same problem will occupy all of this book.

The first three of the five chapters which make up the book will discuss Near Eastern texts and the Theogony. While chapter one covers old as well as new ground, we shall thereafter find ourselves widening the scope of our investigations as we consider the case, first for Babylonian influence on the Theogony in the eighth century B.C., and then for Egyptian influence on the Mycenaean Greeks. In chapter four we shall turn from cosmogony and the story of the gods in order to survey didactic literature in the Near East and Greece, and here Homer will join Hesiod as a source of evidence. Finally, in chapter five, by posing the general question of Hesiod's date, I shall attempt to suggest the route by which a knowledge of Near Eastern ideas reached the mainland of Greece not long before the poet's own lifetime.

There is, however, one difficulty which must first be mentioned: our text of Hesiod has been exposed to the attacks of several generations of critics, and much of it has at different times been assigned to the hand of later poets. The authenticity of individual passages can best be assessed as the passages themselves come under our scrutiny. But also significant is the structure of a poem regarded as a single unit of composition. While comments on the contents and structure of the Works and Days may be deferred until the fourth chapter of the book, it is my intention to state my views on the structure of the Theogony in what remains of the Introduction, so that we can plunge boldly *in medias res* at the beginning of chapter one.

It is doubtful whether anyone today would accept as the original Theogony the text of the poem published in 1930 by Felix Jacoby. Many, nevertheless, reject this or that passage, and some would question the authenticity of certain episodes. What we must do, therefore, is to trace the sequence of events in the Theogony to see if any pattern emerges. The Theogony opens with a prelude to the Muses (verses 1–115); then we read of the coming into existence of Gaia and the birth of the first generation of the gods (verses 116–53); next we have the first 'story' in the Theogony, an account of the castration of Ouranos by Kronos and the appearance of Aphrodite (verses 154–210). After catalogues of the descendants of Night, Pontos, Tethys, Theia, and Phoibe and a hymn to Hekate (verses 211–452), Hesiod relates his second story, how Zeus was safely born and replaced Kronos as king of the gods (verses 453–506). A list of the sons of Iapetos introduces the third story in the poem, that of Prometheus (verses 507–616), and this is followed directly by the Titanomachia or fourth story (verses 617–720). A description of Tartarus (verses 721–819) precedes the story of the clash between Zeus and Typhoeus (verses 820–80). The Theogony ends with a brief reference to the election of Zeus as king (verses 881–5) and a much longer series of marriages or liaisons, headed by those of Zeus (verses 886 ff.).

My summary of contents has been short, but this does not prevent one from seeing how Hesiod skilfully alternates stories and non-dramatic material. There are five stories in the Theogony, the first two of which tell of the struggle for succession and the last two of the battles waged by Zeus in order to confirm his supremacy. It has long been recognized that the story of Ouranos and Kronos and the story of Kronos and Zeus are variations of the same theme: verbal coincidences in the Titanomachia and the story of Typhoeus have not gone unnoticed, although they have often been taken as evidence of the faulty technique of an interpolator. The fact that they are parallel in content shows that the first and last two stories in the Theogony form pairs of stories; the stories which comprise the pairs are separated from one another by a non-dramatic intermezzo, one offering genealogical information and the other describing the underworld.[2] It is only the story of Prometheus which stands by itself, and it is significant that it stands at the climax of the poem with the other stories grouped in pairs symmetrically on either side of it. It is this arrangement of stories which holds the Theogony together and gives it its unity of structure. Because of it I believe we are wrong to reject any of the main episodes in the Theogony or to reduce them drastically in length. The occasional passage may always be suspect, but there is no reason why we should adopt a recent suggestion and exclude from our text the description of Tartarus in verses 736 to 819, the story of Typhoeus, and much of what follows verse 885, including everything after verse 964.[3]

Chapter I

THE THEOGONY AND THE
HITTITE MATERIAL

THE obvious place to commence any study of Hesiod and the literature of the ancient Near East is with the Hittite material. It is no exaggeration to say that the publication of texts and translations of the Hittite Kumarbi and Ullikummi myths has revolutionized our knowledge of the Near Eastern background of Hesiod's Theogony.[1] The tablets which have preserved these texts for us were recovered from the archives of the Hittite capital Hattusas beside the modern Turkish village of Boghazköy, and they date from the period 1400 to 1200 B.C. The actual title of the Kumarbi story is unknown, but it has become customary to refer to it as the Kingship in Heaven myth. This text was known before the Second World War, and Franz Dornseiff was able to comment on it, although only briefly, in his evaluation of oriental elements in the Theogony.[2] The possibility that some connection existed between the contents of the Theogony and the Kumarbi myth seems to have aroused little enthusiasm at that time, for in the first edition of his history of Greek religion Nilsson thought the suggestion worth a bare mention and was content to utter a word of warning, arguing that there were bigger differences than similarities.[3] Nevertheless, things are very much changed today, thanks mainly to the work of Hans G. Güterbock, the most productive of the scholars responsible for reconstructing the text of the Kumarbi and Ullikummi myths and demonstrating their relevance to the problem of Hesiod's sources.[4] Although the revised edition of the Kumarbi myth promised by Güterbock has yet to appear, his latest views on the Kingship in Heaven text are expressed in his chapter on Hittite mythology in Kramer's symposium volume, *Mythologies of the Ancient World*.[5] A new version of the companion myth, the Song of Ullikummi, was published by Güterbock over ten years ago.[6]

The Kingship in Heaven text presents us with many problems, nearly all of which stem from the fact that we have only the one basic copy, itself in a deplorable condition. There are four columns of text, but only the first half of column one is really clear, so that little, apart from

1

the beginning of the story, can be made out. Its significance for the
Theogony will best be appreciated if I summarize the contents of
the myth. After a short introduction which calls on various gods,
including 'primeval deities', to pay heed, we learn that the first king
of heaven was the god Alalu. He reigned for nine 'counted' years, and
was then defeated in battle by mighty Anu and 'went down to the
Dark Earth', leaving Anu on the throne. It was now this god's turn to
be king for nine years, while Kumarbi occupied the subordinate
position that had been Anu's before. But, like Alalu, Anu found
his supremacy challenged by his cup-bearer; unable to withstand
Kumarbi's eyes, he 'went up to the sky' with his rival in furious pursuit.
Kumarbi, seizing Anu by his feet, pulled him down from the sky and
bit off his sexual organs, which he proceeded to swallow. As a result
Anu's manhood united with Kumarbi's interior, as bronze is formed
by the fusion of copper and tin. Next Anu addressed Kumarbi, telling
him that his pleasure at having swallowed his predecessor's manhood
was ill advised, for Kumarbi had thus become impregnated with five
deities, the Storm-god, the river Tigris, the god Tashmishu (the
attendant and helper of the Storm-god), and two other terrible gods,
perhaps Marduk and 'lust', who appear in the second column. Kumarbi
responded by spitting out of his mouth a mixture, presumably of spittle
and the genitals of Anu. Kumarbi then retired angrily to Nippur and
nine months passed. It is at this point that the first column of the text
breaks off.

It is extremely difficult to establish what followed in the narrative.
In column two several gods, two of whom are Marduk and 'lust',
appear to be inside Kumarbi and are anxious to find a way out, and
so they discuss with Kumarbi what route they are to take. A fragment
on which the Storm-god talks to Anu may fill the gap between the
second and third columns: the third column may open with the
Storm-god asking Anu to kill Kumarbi. Further speeches from Anu
and the Storm-god follow and the god Ea is introduced into the story,
perhaps as the result of a proposal made by Anu that Ea become king.
In column four Earth produces two children, but it is impossible to
identify either them or their father. All this is very puzzling, and one
hardly knows where to begin trying to piece such scraps of information
together. The Storm-god ranked as the supreme god of the Hittite
pantheon, and it can be assumed that the Kumarbi myth must have
related not only how the Storm-god came to be born but also his
elevation to the throne of heaven. But how exactly that event was fitted

into the story again it is impossible to say. Indeed, until another copy of the myth is made available, we are not likely to progress much further and achieve a fuller understanding of what happened after the castration of Anu by Kumarbi.

One link, however, with the story told by Hesiod in his Theogony is plain, for we encounter in the Hittite tradition a number of successive dynasties of the gods which recall Hesiod's sequence Ouranos, Kronos, and Zeus. But no one can be certain as to the number of divine kings featured in the Kingship in Heaven text. We do know that there were Alalu, Anu, and Kumarbi, and to these we must add the Storm-god himself, while the rule of Ea is also a possibility. The gods are related to each other just as their Greek opposites are: if we ignore the evidence which can be adduced from other sources, in the Kingship in Heaven text Kumarbi is called the offspring of Alalu, and it is a combination of Anu and Kumarbi which gives birth to the Storm-god. The two groups of gods, Hittite and Greek, moreover, correspond, for Anu is 'Heaven', while, in a Hurrian text from Ras Shamra, the ancient Ugarit, Kumarbi is identified with El, a god whom Philo of Byblos makes the Phoenician equivalent of the Greek Kronos.[7] The Storm-god and Zeus are the supreme gods among the Hittites and Greeks respectively.

But to what extent can we press other parallels? One suggestion of earlier years, that we have in the Kumarbi myth an incident which parallels Hesiod's story of how Kronos swallowed a stone as a substitute for his son Zeus (Theogony, 485 ff.), appears now to have been dropped by Güterbock, who does not refer to it in *Mythologies*.[8] If, in the second column of the Hittite text, Kumarbi attempted to eat a child and there was mention of a cult connected with a stone fetish, the analogy with the story of Kronos and Zeus in the Theogony would be striking. Güterbock, however, has never denied how difficult it is to extract a continuous narrative from the damaged part of the Hittite text, and there is a strong reason why it is very hard to believe that Kumarbi wanted to consume one of his children, for, when the Hittite and Greek stories are compared, the situation is seen to be totally different. Kronos, according to Hesiod, used his own body as a prison in which he kept locked away offspring already born and then swallowed by their father. He was supplied with a stone substitute to prevent this happening to Zeus; the stone served as a trick which deceived Kronos. Kumarbi, on the other hand, was impregnated with children yet to see the light of day, and the difficulty here is to get the Storm-god

safely out of Kumarbi and not to stop his getting in. The Storm-god
had to be born, and that was not going to be easy when the person
pregnant was a male and not a female. It was necessary for Kumarbi
to free himself of the burden present in his vitals, and I cannot see how
this was to be achieved if he added to his troubles by swallowing
another child. If Kumarbi did receive something to eat in column two,
then a drug to act as an emetic and thus to accelerate the process of
childbirth meets the logical requirements of the story better than
anything else. A stone, I suppose, could be used as an emetic, and it is
possible, therefore, that Hesiod's stone may go back ultimately to
Hittite tradition, but if it does, the idea behind the motif has been
changed, since the stone in the Theogony has no effect on Kronos and
is certainly not depicted as a purge of any kind.

We shall have to return later to the stone. For the moment let us
consider another detail where our Hittite and Greek stories appear to
coincide. Anu suffers emasculation at the hands of Kumarbi and,
strange though it may seem, children are consequently produced. After
the attack on Anu one has to deal with the damaged portion of the
Kingship in Heaven text where everything is highly speculative and
conclusions, at best, provisional. But it would appear that the birth of
the Storm-god and others was recorded in the second column. Towards
the end of the myth Earth gives birth to a pair of children. Column one
is a long way from column four, but let us admit the possibility that
here we have an account of what befell the part of the seed which
Kumarbi managed to eject: the god spat it out and Earth received it,
and so in time she bore two children. Can it be argued that this is
substantially the same story as that told by Hesiod when he describes
how Kronos came to overthrow his father Ouranos?

The poet's story needs only a brief description: Ouranos did violence
to his children, thrusting them away in the earth (verses 156 ff.). His
act caused Gaia distress, and she concealed their son Kronos in an
ambush, placing in his hands a great sickle. When Ouranos lay with
Gaia, Kronos stretched out and used the weapon to sever Ouranos'
male parts. Kronos threw the genitals away behind him, and Gaia
received the drops of blood from them, in due course giving birth to the
Erinyes, Giants, and Melian Nymphs. The actual genitals were cast
into the sea, and in the white foam which spread about them was
nurtured the goddess Aphrodite (verses 188–92). In the Kumarbi myth
and the Theogony, therefore, 'Heaven' is castrated and new deities
come into existence: Earth in the Theogony is the mother of the

Erinyes, Giants, and Melian Nymphs, and there is a chance – but, I must stress, only a chance – that in the Kumarbi myth Earth was made pregnant in something like the same way.

There are also differences between the two stories, and some may regard these as more impressive. It seems that Anu, although mutilated, still has much to do in the Hittite story, whereas Hesiod's Ouranos, once he has been dispossessed of his throne, plays a passive role, merely issuing warnings or being available for advice (verses 463–5 and 888 ff., and 468 ff.). As we have been seeing, Kronos is not left with gods inside him waiting to be born. That later in the Theogony Kronos swallows his own offspring is no parallel, for they have already been born and Kronos, well aware of what he is doing, is consciously trying to suppress a threat to the continuance of his power. There is, furthermore, no obvious connection between the offspring enumerated in the two stories. Hesiod's collection is a curious mixture, and one wonders what made him join together Erinyes, Giants, and Melian Nymphs. Some fanciful answers have been proposed, but, in my opinion, the problem remains to be solved.[9] The nature of her birth puts Aphrodite in a separate category, and it is not surprising that a few have classed this passage as an interpolation. But the suggestion is surely absurd, since the Theogony would then contain no record of the birth of so important a deity, a deity, moreover, who is included in the first catalogue of the poem (verse 16). Indeed two other passages in the Theogony confirm the authenticity of Hesiod's description of Aphrodite, and one of these helps us to understand the significance of Aphrodite's birth, making it clear that the Kumarbi myth offers no true parallel.

Hesiod's reference to Perseus and the beheading of Medusa (verses 280 ff.) repeats the same theme, birth following an act of dismemberment, as the description of Aphrodite, and corresponds exactly in structure. From the severed head of Medusa there bounded forth Chrysaor and Pegasos, whose names are etymologized, as were those of Aphrodite (cf. verses 195–200 and 282–3). Pegasos arrived among the immortals, again like Aphrodite (cf. verses 201–2 and 284–5), and, yet again like the goddess, was allocated a special task, carrying the thunder and lightning for Zeus (cf. verses 203–6 and 285–6). One scholar has recognized Anatolian features in the Perseus myth.[10] We also have evidence for a Babylonian tradition according to which Anu has his neck cut off.[11] One detail in Hesiod's story of Aphrodite's birth can be explained only in terms of Near Eastern influence, though it is Mesopotamian rather than Hittite influence: unlike Homer, Hesiod makes Aphrodite a daughter of Ouranos and not of Zeus; in the same way the goddess Ishtar was thought to be the daughter of Anu and Antum, so that, for example, in the Epic of Gilgamesh Ishtar, having been brutally rejected by the hero, requires her father Anu to fashion the Bull of Heaven and so let her have her revenge.

The castration of Ouranos represents the separation of heaven and earth, and it repeats what Hesiod has already described when we read that first Chaos, a gap, came into being and next Earth (verses 116 ff.).[12] The dismemberment of Ouranos is followed by the birth of Aphrodite, one of whose companions is Eros (verse 201). But Eros has put in an appearance before, immediately after the production of Chaos, where we find listed in order of appearance Earth and Eros.[13] The fact that this force is made to appear with Gaia explains why its mythopoeic equivalent Aphrodite should be born after the same act of separation, this time expressed by the castration of Ouranos. This interpretation of the birth of Aphrodite gives the goddess a particular significance not to be found in the Kingship in Heaven text.

Only two analogies, I think, between the Theogony and the Kingship in Heaven text can be accepted, and neither of these is as simple as one might imagine at first sight: if we allow the possibility that at some stage or another Ea assumed control, the Hittite story of the dynasties of the gods is more complex than is often admitted; the castration motif, when the two versions are compared, reveals differences as well as similarities. Yet nobody would want to argue that Hesiod composed the Theogony with the Hittite text open in front of him, for something like half a millennium separates the tablets from Hattusas from the approximate date when the Theogony was composed. Can we expect much more than the outline of both stories to be the same? But there is a greater difficulty: whatever happens in detail after the disposal of Anu in the Kumarbi myth, it seems to be very different from the events following the castration of Ouranos. Whenever lavish claims are advanced in support of a close relationship between Hesiod and the Hittite material, I cannot help asking myself what parallels scholars would have been able to develop if fate had preserved for us in a reasonable shape any part of the Kumarbi myth other than its beginning. Am I being unfair if I say that in those circumstances a connection with the Theogony would have been considerably less obvious? One can, I think, even go as far as saying that it might not have been at all evident. This is one of the reasons why I suggested in the Introduction

that scholars have been overhasty when discussing Hesiod and his debt
to Near Eastern sources.

The text of our other Hittite myth is much easier to examine, for we
have several copies, and, with the exception of its conclusion and an
occasional break, it is possible to reconstruct the whole narrative. We
know its title was the Song of Ullikummi. It appears to carry on with
the story of the struggle between Kumarbi and the Storm-god, the
latter now being king of heaven. At its beginning we read, 'Of Kumarbi,
father of all gods, I shall sing'. It goes on to relate how Kumarbi
plotted evil against Teshub the Storm-god and provided a challenger
to his throne; he did this by fertilizing a rock which gave birth to the
stone monster Ullikummi. The monster's name of Ulli-kummi is a play
on the task he was to undertake, namely the destruction of Kummiya,
the residence of the Storm-god. Indeed Ullikummi was to 'hit Teshub
and pound him like chaff and crush him with his foot like an ant'.
When the child was delivered, it was placed on Kumarbi's knees,
a detail we shall see later in the story of Appu (p. 99) and one also to
be found in the Theogony (cf. verse 460). Ullikummi grew up, planted
on the right shoulder of Ubelluri, an Atlas type of giant who carried
heaven and earth. The monster soon reached a prodigious size with its
head touching the sky, while the sea stopped short at its waist. The
Sun-god brought news of his rival to Teshub, who, accompanied by
Tashmishu and their sister Ishtar, went to Mount Hazzi where the three
of them surveyed 'the dreadful Stone'.

At first Teshub was overwhelmed with fear by the sight of Ullikummi,
but, after an episode where Ishtar tried unsuccessfully to deploy her
charms against the monster, Teshub had his war-chariot prepared.
The battle which resulted, however, went in favour of his opponent,
and Ullikummi was able to threaten Kummiya and to endanger the
Storm-god's consort, the goddess Hebat. When Tashmishu told Hebat
that her husband would have to surrender his sovereignty for the time
being, the queen's reaction was violent:

> When Hebat saw Tashmishu
> she almost fell from the roof.
> Had she taken a step,
> she would have fallen from the roof,
> but the palace women held her and let her not go.

It was left to the god Ea to find a solution: he visited Ubelluri, and the
Hittite Atlas claimed that, as he had noticed nothing when Heaven
and Earth were built on him and then when they were cut apart, so at

the moment he was conscious of discomfort in his right shoulder, but had no idea who was causing it. It is, of course, Ullikummi. Next Ea ordered the 'Former Gods' to produce the cutting tool with which Heaven and Earth had originally been separated; this instrument seems to have been employed to separate Ullikummi from the shoulder of Ubelluri, thus destroying the power of the monster; then we find Ea urging Tashmishu to renew the war. The gods reassembled and Teshub and Ullikummi fought again. Apart from scraps of a conversation between the two opposing champions, the end of the myth is lost, but here, as in the Kumarbi myth, we may assume that the outcome of this second action left Teshub undisputed king of the gods. The odd piece of information can be extremely valuable. Thus we learn from Ubelluri's words to Ea that Heaven and Earth were first built on Ubelluri, but later separated with some kind of cutting tool, of which the 'Former Gods' took charge. So bald a reference does not tell us much, but one thinks of the sickle Kronos used to castrate Ouranos. The text defines neither the past nor the present status of the 'Former Gods', although their name in itself suggests a group not unlike the Titans, forced to surrender their authority to a new generation of the gods.[14]

It is a great pity that we do not have more of the final exchange between Teshub and Ullikummi, so that we may see with what justification Güterbock calls it 'an almost Homeric dialogue'.[15] A number of interesting reminiscences of the Song of Ullikummi have been identified in the Homeric poems. Thus Webster has compared Hera's chariot in Iliad v, 720 ff. and the preparation of Teshub's chariot; he also points out how Andromache reacts like Hebat and falls back fainting when she sees her husband's body being dragged by Achilles' horses (Iliad xxii, 462 ff.).[16] The second suggestion is strengthened by the researches of Kardara, who is tempted 'to see behind the epic Andromache a local deity of Anatolia, a warlike goddess, either Hittite or Hurrian'.[17] Before Webster Albin Lesky had explained Homer's description of Atlas in Odyssey i, 52–4 by reference to Ubelluri, and had noted that both in Homer and our Hittite myth the gods rise in respect when a superior enters.[18] This last similarity, however, reveals the risks we are likely to run if we compare isolated details. To stand up as a token of respect is a widespread habit and far from being peculiar to the Ullikummi story and Homer. A classic example is offered by the Babylonian myth of Nergal and Ereshkigal as we know it from a text recovered at Tell el-Amarna in Egypt, which dates from the fourteenth century B.C.[19] Here Nergal gravely offends the goddess of the under-world, Ereshkigal, by remaining seated when all the gods rise at the arrival in heaven of her envoy Namtar. The excavations at Sultantepe have led to the discovery of a Late Assyrian version of the same myth. In this text Nergal's crime has been changed from a failure to rise to a failure to kneel before the envoy of the goddess.[20] It is important to note that the Sultantepe tablet is about five times as long as the earlier version, and represents a much more elaborate and literary treatment of the story. Unless the Tell el-Amarna text is a local abbreviated edition, here we have some indication of what could happen to a myth in the course of time. The two versions of the myth of Nergal and Ereshkigal, like our various treatments of the Gilgamesh story, give the classical specialist an idea of the gulf which separates Homer and Hesiod from possible handling of the same basic raw material by Mycenaean singers.[21]

Apart from a few breaks we can trace the story told in the Song of Ullikummi from its beginning to almost its end. We are, therefore, in a much better position in the case of this text to assess the link between it and the Theogony. I have always felt the results to be more than a little disappointing. Ullikummi is thought to correspond with Hesiod's Typhoeus. Having defeated the Titans, Zeus faced a new menace in the person of Typhoeus, admittedly a different type of monster with a hundred snake-heads growing from its shoulders, but still a monster which it took all of Zeus' strength to subdue (verses 820 ff.). The Kumarbi and Ullikummi myths are separate compositions, but, if we are right to couple them together as parts of the same cycle of myths, it can be said that both the struggle against Typhoeus and the struggle against Ullikummi occupy the same position in the general scheme of the narrative: both are an attempt to overthrow the new king of heaven after he had gained the throne by the defeat of his predecessor. The rest of the Theogony and the battle with Typhoeus go together as much as our two Hittite myths go together. This has important consequences with regard to the authenticity of the Typhoeus episode: it should help us to justify its retention as part of the original composition of the Theogony in face of nearly universal condemnation, for it implies that this type of myth included both the story of the different generations of the gods, culminating in the accession of Zeus or some equivalent figure, and a final clash between the supreme god and a monstrous rival. Hesiod's account of Typhoeus then becomes an essential part of

the Theogony, and is no longer a tiresome repetition of the Titanomachia added by a clumsy interpolator. There are some, however, who
accept that the story of Typhoeus originated in the Near East but are
still convinced that it does not form part of the Theogony as Hesiod
composed that poem. We need evidence to show beyond dispute that
the Kumarbi and Ullikummi stories should be taken together as distinct
episodes in the same cycle of myths, and this evidence we do not
possess at present. Although many have scrutinized the language in
Hesiod's description of the fight between Zeus and Typhoeus, arguments based on linguistic evidence have proved indecisive in settling the
problem of authenticity. One critic is able to demolish the theory of
Hesiodic authorship, while another, ten years later, affirms that the
passage is authentic Hesiod.[22] I can only refer back to the Introduction
and argue that we must retain the story of Typhoeus if we are to allow
the Theogony any kind of structural pattern: the first half of the poem
relates two parallel stories which describe the struggle for the throne
of heaven, while its second half consists, in the main, of two matching
descriptions of the battles by which Zeus consolidated his position as
king.

The setting of the Song of Ullikummi is localized in North Syria and
Cilicia. The gods repair to Mount Hazzi to get a look at Ullikummi,
and Mount Hazzi is the classical Mons Casius, located in North Syria
just to the south of the mouth of the Orontes river.[23] According to
Güterbock, in a cuneiform text as yet unpublished, Ullikummi is the
name of a mountain in Cilicia.[24] Where, if anywhere, does Hesiod fix
the scene of his battle between Zeus and Typhoeus? In the fifth
century B.C. Aeschylus calls Typhon, a variant on the Hesiodic name,
the earth-born dweller of the Cilician caves (Prometheus Vinctus,
351 ff.), and Pindar says that the Cilician cave reared him (Pyth. 1,
16–7; cf. Pyth. 8, 16).[25] Herodotus associates Typhon with Mons
Casius but not the Syrian mountain of that name. He refers to another
Mons Casius beside Lake Serbonis on the borders of Egypt and
Palestine, where Typhon, he reports, was reputed to lie hidden (3, 5,
2–3). All that Hesiod has to offer on the habitat of Typhoeus comes
early in the Theogony, when we read that Typhaon, yet another form
of the same name, was said to have mated with an equally loathsome
creature, Echidna, who lived in a cave 'among the Arimoi' (verses
301 ff.). The passage comes from a section of the Theogony which has
received a very bad press, usually for reasons flattering to Hesiod: the
difficulty we have in referring relatives to their antecedents, as in

verses 295, 319, and 326, is the mark of an inferior poet and therefore
not Hesiod; the vague 'they say' of verse 306 implies a degree of
ignorance of which Hesiod's Muses could never be guilty. But such
arguments may well be thought trivial. Homer's only reference to
Typhoeus comes in a simile in Iliad ii, 781–3 when the advancing
Greeks caused the earth to groan mightily beneath their feet, as it does
when Zeus in his fury lashes the earth about Typhoeus 'among the
Arimoi', though here we have the phrase expanded by the statement
'where they say the couches of Typhoeus are'. It is impossible to say
what the formula 'among the Arimoi' meant for Homer and Hesiod,
and I prefer to take the side of the majority and argue that neither poet
has any precise geographical setting in mind when he uses it. After all,
Hesiod does say in verse 302 that Echidna's cave is far removed from
gods and men, and this I find it hard to associate with a definite spot
on the map. At a much later period the geographer Strabo in referring
to the Arimoi notes that changes of names, especially in the case of
those of barbarian peoples, are frequent (16, 785), and he himself
shows that there was no common opinion as to where the Arimoi were
to be located (cf. 12, 579; 13, 626–8; and 16, 750).[26]

In the Budé edition of Hesiod Mazon has an interesting suggestion to
make in his note on verse 860 of the Theogony. In that line the proper
name Etna has often been mistakenly read (for $ἀιδνῆς$). But one feels
the need for a specific reference, and so Mazon suggests that the
unnamed mountain mentioned here is a mountain situated in Boeotia.
This means that it is a landmark familiar to the poet's audience and its
name may be omitted. The evidence for a mountain in Boeotia connected with Zeus' victory over Typhoeus is supplied by verse 32 of
the Aspis, a part of the poem which, according to one of the hypotheses
attached to it, was included in the fourth book of the Catalogue. Here
we learn how Zeus, inflamed with passion for Alkmene, arose from
Olympus at night and quickly came to Typhaonion; from there he went
on to the top of Phikion. All three places appear to be mountains.
Phikion seems to owe its name to the Sphinx (cf. Theogony, 326), while
Typhaonion suggests the dragon Typhoeus. Phikion is the end of the
journey for Zeus and must, therefore, stand near Thebes. Late authori-
ties have led some to assume that Typhaonion is also to be found in
Boeotia.[27] If Mazon's theory is adopted, then one has to abandon any
idea of a Cilician setting for Hesiod's story of Typhoeus. But, as usual,
there are difficulties to make us pause: first we must believe that who-
ever was responsible for the description of Zeus' journey in the Aspis

was employing an actual route from Olympus to Thebes; if that is acceptable, we can still positively identify only the two limits of the journey, and Mount Typhaonion, whatever late sources may say, is to be placed anywhere between them.[28]

I hope it will now be appreciated why I said earlier that a comparison of the Theogony and the Song of Ullikummi produces disappointing results. It is true that both poems (the Song of Ullikummi, as its name indicates, is a poem) tell how the last king of the gods was challenged by a monster whose efforts to displace the king proved abortive, but this is the one parallel between them. Nevertheless, we are far from being finished with the Hittite material, since it is possible to detect the influence of motifs going back to Hittite sources in Greek authors long after Homer and Hesiod. Such influence survives at a remarkably late date and in the most unexpected forms. A good example comes in a scholiast's note on the Homeric reference to Typhoeus which I quoted a short while ago. The B-scholion presents us with a story which relates how Hera, at the instigation of Gaia, enlisted the aid of Kronos against her husband Zeus. Kronos gave Hera two eggs smeared with his own semen, and told the goddess to bury them underground, for from the eggs would be produced a force capable of supplanting Zeus. Hera followed these instructions and buried the eggs under 'Arimon of Cilicia'. But when, as a result, Typhon appeared, Hera was once more on friendly terms with Zeus and revealed all; Zeus then destroyed Typhon with his thunderbolt and gave the mountain the name Etna! Although the last detail adds a garbled touch to the story, the intervention of Hera was part of the Typhoeus tradition as early as the composition of the second part of the Hymn to Apollo, for that poem describes how Hera gave birth to the monster, without male assistance, in order to match the birth of Athene from Zeus (verses 305 ff.). The scholiast's story makes Kronos the parent of Typhon, just as Kumarbi was the father of Ullikummi, and it reminds us as well of the process by which Kumarbi produced Ullikummi, by sleeping with a rock into which his virility poured. The version of the Typhoeus story preserved by Apollodorus reinforces an impression that material could survive the passage of centuries. Apollodorus follows Hesiod in making Gaia the mother of Typhon (1, 6, 3). Typhon was of incredible size, towering over the mountain tops and often knocking against the stars. His appearance on the scene was enough to send the gods rushing off to Egypt, but Zeus, who was made of sterner stuff, stood firm and put up a resistance, using thunderbolts as long-range weapons and a sickle for fighting at close quarters. At first he did well and chased his foe to Mons Casius, but then he made a mistake: he grappled with Typhon, who enmeshed the god in his coils and wrestled the sickle away from Zeus. Typhon used the sickle to cut through the sinews of Zeus' hands and feet. Stripped of his sinews, Zeus was helpless, and both he and the sinews were deposited by Typhon in the Corycian cave. But Hermes and Aigipan recovered the sinews and fitted them back on Zeus. His strength now restored, Zeus tackled his enemy again. Typhon's ability to resist was undermined when the Fates deceived him into eating what Apollodorus calls 'the ephemeral fruits'. Pursued by Zeus, he fled to Thrace and then went on to Sicily, where Zeus heaped Mount Etna on top of him.

A new element in Apollodorus' account of the defeat of Typhon is the part ascribed to the Fates. Another detail for which there is no immediate parallel comes earlier when the mythographer describes how Kronos used to swallow his newly born children. Zeus avoided this fate and Kronos was supplied with a stone substitute. When Zeus attained manhood, he took Metis as an accomplice, and the goddess administered a drug to Kronos which compelled him to disgorge the stone and the children he had swallowed (1, 2, 1). To appreciate the significance of both of these details, we must, I think, take another look at the Hittite tradition. The drug which Metis gave to Kronos is suspiciously like something intended to hasten or facilitate the act of birth, and here, as I have shown before (pp. 3–4), we appear to have an incident which fits into the narrative of the Kumarbi myth much better than it does into that of the story of Kronos. The same idea seems to lie behind a reference made by Nonnus, an author of whom I shall have more to say later in this chapter. In the forty-first book of the Dionysiaca, a book where the influence of Phoenician mythology has been detected by Eissfeldt,[29] Nonnus mentions that the city of Beroe (i.e. Beirut) was built by Kronos at the time when he was persuaded by Rhea to swallow a stone which caused him to disgorge his sons, who were thus born twice, once in the normal fashion and later from out of their father's throat (verses 68–76). The stone is explicitly said to act as a deliverer, and there is no suggestion that it was designed to substitute for baby Zeus; in fact, Zeus is not even mentioned until the following passage. In the Theogony time passes after the stone has been eaten so that Zeus can grow up (cf. verses 492–3), whereas Nonnus' stone goes into action as soon as it has been swallowed and the results are devastating: Kronos gulps down a whole river in an attempt to check the pain and the children come pouring out. Nonnus' sense of chronology is woefully confused, for, after this reference to Kronos and his children, he goes on to expatiate on the antiquity of Beroe, claiming, among other things, that it was at Beroe that Aphrodite first stepped ashore (verses 97 ff.). His logic is equally defective, and in other passages he follows the orthodox tradition and makes the stone a substitute for Zeus (xxviii, 322–3) or conflates the motifs of substitute and emetic by having the stone act in both capacities (xii, 48–51 and xxv, 553–62).

To understand what the ephemeral fruits mean, it is necessary to turn to another Hittite myth. This tells the story of a struggle between the Storm-god and, this time, not a monster of stone but an authentic dragon. Two versions of the myth of the Illuyanka are preserved on the same tablet.[30] According to one, the earlier version we learn from the text, the Storm-god and the dragon fought and the former was defeated. A great feast was then organized, to which the goddess Inara invited the dragon and his brood. So well did they celebrate and so much drink was consumed that they were rendered incapable of returning to their lair. A mortal man whose aid was enlisted by Inara seized the opportunity to bind the dragon, and it was thereupon killed by the Storm-god. Thus, as the ephemeral fruits sap the strength of Typhon, so do food and drink contribute to the downfall of the Illuyanka. Oppian of Cilicia also suggests influence ultimately derived from the first version of the Illuyanka myth. This poet in his Halieutica reports that Pan of Corycus, the son of Hermes, was called the saviour of Zeus but the destroyer of Typhon. He adds that Pan deceived terrible Typhon with a banquet of fish, persuading him in this way to quit his cave and expose himself on the seashore to an attack from Zeus (iii, 15–25).[31]

The other version of the Illuyanka myth is relevant to our investigations, since it depicts the Storm-god made powerless by the loss of vital organs. Again it opens with the defeat of the Storm-god, from whom the dragon removed heart and eyes. The god retaliated by begetting a son by a mortal woman; on becoming a man, the son married the daughter of the dragon and succeeded in acquiring his father's heart and eyes by demanding them as the bride-price. They were handed over to the Storm-god, who was then able to defeat the dragon. We have already seen that Apollodorus records the loss of Zeus' sinews (p. 13). Comparable is a tradition preserved by Nonnus in the Dionysiaca, although his reference to the sinews is a casual one. Nonnus relates how Zeus, off on one of his amorous adventures, left his thunderbolts and lightning behind but was careful to conceal them deep in a cave (i, 145 ff.). But he was not careful enough, for Cilician Typhoeus was able to steal them. Once in possession of the weapons of Zeus, Typhoeus ran wild until a mortal, Kadmos, dressed up as a rustic and given a set of pipes, was sent by Zeus to beguile Typhoeus (verses 363 ff.). The dragon had a taste for music and, hearing Kadmos' pipes, invited him to provide more entertainment. Kadmos, however, told Typhoeus that his piping was nothing compared to his accomplishments on the lyre, but that he had had the temerity to vanquish Apollo in a musical contest and Zeus had destroyed his strings to gratify Apollo (verses 486 ff.). If he was to play his lyre again, Kadmos had to have sinews as a replacement; Typhoeus obliged him by hurrying away to his cave and producing from that place the sinews of Zeus, which he gave to Kadmos. At this point in the story Nonnus adds, by way of explanation, that the sinews had fallen to the ground during the struggle with Typhoeus (verses 510–2). Kadmos, having hidden the sinews away so as to keep them safe for Zeus, started on his pipes again and held the dragon's attention while Zeus crept into his den and recovered his own weapons. The story told by Nonnus would run smoothly without any mention of the sinews of Zeus, for what we need is Typhoeus entranced while the god gets his thunderbolts back. The sinews are introduced abruptly into the story and we have a lame explanation appended to account for Typhoeus' possession of them. Unlike Apollodorus who makes the loss of sinews an integral part of his plot, Nonnus hurries over this, strictly speaking, superfluous detail without seeming to appreciate its true import.

It appears that the two engagements between god and dragon in the second story of the Illuyanka took place by the sea.[32] This suggests the same kind of location by Mons Casius that we meet in the case of the first battle in both the Song of Ullikummi and Apollodorus' story of Typhon. Other details in Apollodorus, such as the colossal size of Typhon and Zeus' use of a sickle as a weapon, find parallels in the Song of Ullikummi. Oppian makes the seashore the place where Typhon met his doom. But how are we to explain the fact that our text of Apollodorus and Oppian seems to include details which are best understood if we refer not to Greek but to Hittite mythology? The period of time which separates Apollodorus from the Hittite myths we have discussed is immense, comprising as it does a thousand and more years, while Oppian and Nonnus are even later in date. The chances of oral transmission are remote and not what we should expect, knowing the methods of the compiler of the Library. Two possibilities are worth considering, and, if we next look at them in turn, I think it will help us to clarify the relationship between Hesiod and the literature of the Near East. The first possibility is that an author such as Apollodorus took advantage of the work of Hellenistic scholars who studied and translated texts current at the time when great empires controlled the Near East. Famous names like those of Manetho and Berossus in themselves reveal that Hellenistic culture was no one-way traffic with the Greeks supplying everything and the Orient nothing. Berossus, for example, was conversant with the story of the flood and a version of the Babylonian creation legend. Alternatively, it is possible that elements derived from the Near East entered Greek tradition at an altogether earlier date. Let us concentrate, however, for the moment on the first possibility.

I imagine that few will want to quarrel with me when I say that of all the poems which survive today from the ancient Near East the Epic of Gilgamesh is the one we enjoy most. It is difficult to believe that a wide knowledge of it vanished with the destruction of the Assyrian empire. There is one passage from the poem which, I have always felt, would have appealed enormously to Hellenistic tastes. This is the episode where Gilgamesh rejects the advances of the goddess Ishtar and catalogues her lovers of former days.[33] His account of their fate at the hands of Ishtar makes sorry reading. Tammuz, the lover of her youth, has been left an object for annual lamentation. The dappled shepherd-bird had its wing broken by the goddess, while Ishtar dug a whole series of pits to ensnare the mighty lion she once adored. Her next victim was a stallion and he is now reduced to enduring the whip, spur, and lash; he is made to gallop seven leagues and drink muddied water. She selected the keeper of the herd as another object of her dangerous affection, and in the end he was transformed into a wolf and was assailed by his own helpers and dogs. Ishullanu, the gardener, resembled Gilgamesh in spurning Ishtar's offers of love, and he was changed into a 'mole'. Gilgamesh, having humiliated Ishtar, is to find himself opposed by the Bull of Heaven.

Those who have discussed the possible influence of this passage on Greek literature have confined their analogies to Homer, comparing either the desertion of Calypso by Odysseus or Circe's transformation of the companions of Odysseus. But, if Ishtar in the Epic of Gilgamesh is to be compared to Circe, it is Ovid's Circe in the Metamorphoses whom we should consider. In the fourteenth book of the Metamorphoses Ovid describes how Circe fell desperately in love with young Picus when she saw him out hunting. She contrived his separation from his fellows and addressed herself to him, revealing her love. Then, after Picus had repelled her, she proceeded to change him into a woodpecker (verses 320 ff.). Ovid's story of Circe and Picus is characteristic of many of the episodes in the Metamorphoses inasmuch as it opens with someone falling in love and ends with an act of metamorphosis. The frequency with which the theme of metamorphosis by itself was adopted by the poets of the Hellenistic age suggests one reason why this passage from the Epic of Gilgamesh should have been popular with literary circles; that it is also connected with the idea of love might well have made it irresistibly attractive. There is, furthermore, a passage in Hellenistic poetry where we encounter a situation not at all unlike that in the Gilgamesh story. This is the first idyll of Theocritus, when the dying Daphnis taunts the goddess Aphrodite (verses 100 ff.). Although the circumstances which cause the goddess of love to reveal herself to Gilgamesh and Daphnis are different, the response she meets from both is identical: both pour forth a passionate torrent of abuse and both quote mythological precedents in order to drive their insults home. Also comparable is the exchange between Aqhat and the goddess Anat in the Ugaritic legend of Aqhat. Anat, in addition, seems to regret having later engineered the death of Aqhat, as Aphrodite, according to one interpretation of the song of Thyrsis, regrets being responsible for the death of Daphnis.[34] We have started to wander far from our main subject, but I think it relevant to note that Near Eastern literature, although few have considered it, is a legitimate field of research if one tries to identify Ovid's source material.[35] This is a huge topic in need of systematic treatment, but all we normally meet is the occasional note. Thus, to quote a recent example, Fontenrose has compared the growth of Ullikummi and Ovid's description of Atlas turned into stone by Perseus (Met. iv, 660–2), while Gadd – and now we turn to another Latin poet – in discussing the survival of the Etana tradition as embodied in the myth of Ganymedes has referred to 'the curiously faithful description in Statius' (Thebaid i, 548–51).[36]

There is fortunately a more positive clue, for we possess a vital piece of information about the material available to Philo of Byblos, an author of approximately the same date as the Library. Fragments of his Phoenician History are preserved by Eusebius in the Praeparatio Evangelica.[37] We learn from Eusebius that Philo translated into Greek the work of a certain Sanchuniathon. Eusebius also quotes Porphyrius on

Sanchuniathon and Philo, and from this it appears that Sanchuniathon, a native of Beirut, 'obtained the records' from a priest with the name of Hierombalos, who, having 'submitted' the history to Abibalos, king of Beirut, was 'accepted' by the king and his experts. Porphyrius, who was able to base his calculations on the list of Phoenician kings, reckoned that these people lived before the Trojan War and near the time of Moses. This is not what we should call a proper chronology, but it presumably indicates a date before the twelfth century B.C. Sanchuniathon seems to have had access to old material from city and temple archives.

The discovery of the texts from Ugarit, which belong to the fourteenth century B.C., has brought about the rehabilitation of Philo and his alleged source, since names occur on the Ugaritic tablets which are similar to those recorded by Philo. As a result it is not so easy today as it has been in the past to cast doubt on the extreme age and authenticity of Philo's material. Especially convincing for the early date of Sanchuniathon is the colophon of a text about Baal where we appear to have the same relationship between scribe, teacher, and patron as that claimed for Sanchuniathon, Hierombalos, and Abibalos:

> Written by Elimelech the Shabnite.
> Dictated by Attani-puruleni, Chief of Priests, Chief of
> Temple-herdsmen.
> Donated by Niqmadd, King of Ugarit, Master of Yargub,
> Lord of Tharumeni.[38]

It is surely reasonable to conclude that Philo did actually translate from Phoenician into Greek a text like those we know from Ugarit, and that his name should, therefore, be added to those of Berossus and his colleagues. Berossus, Philo, and those who produced the Septuagint are all examples of scholars who made the contents of Near Eastern texts available to a Greek-speaking public after Alexander's conquest of the Persian empire.

So far we have been trying to assess our first possibility, namely that it was during the Hellenistic and later period that the literature of the Near East influenced the Greeks. But it is equally possible that such influence was felt long before. There is one mythographer of early date who, like Philo, was reputed to have had access to Phoenician material, and, if we glance now at this author, we shall find our way back to the two Hittite myths with which we began this chapter. The mythographer is Pherecydes of Syros and his date some time in the sixth century B.C. According to Philo, again as quoted by Eusebius, Pherecydes was inspired by Phoenicians when he wrote about the god he called Ophioneus and the Ophionidai.[39] The Suda entry on Pherecydes states that he had no teacher but taught himself, having obtained the secret books of the Phoenicians. Perhaps neither statement is worth much as an isolated piece of evidence, but the little we know in detail about the contents of Pherecydes' book confirms the validity of the claim. Indeed, although our knowledge of Pherecydes' book is scanty, it is remarkable how many parallels between its contents and traditions current in the Near East have been traced.[40] If Pherecydes was influenced by Near Eastern ideas, we should make more of what the Suda and Philo have to say about his dependence on Phoenician sources, and we ought to focus our attention on the general region of Syria and texts associated with peoples active in that area. I am thinking of three distinct types of texts – first the tablets from Ugarit, secondly Philo's work, and last, and here perhaps is the surprise, the Kumarbi and Ullikummi myths.

It is clear why the Ugaritic texts and Philo of Byblos are relevant to the understanding of Pherecydes if the Phoenicians had any influence on him: Ugarit is in North Syria, while Philo translated from the Phoenician. But how can Hittite myths be connected with Syria and, therefore, with Pherecydes? The answer is a simple one. I have called the Kingship in Heaven text and the Song of Ullikummi Hittite myths throughout this chapter, but for one reason alone, because the tablets on which they are preserved contain texts written in the Hittite language. These two myths, however, are of a sophisticated character not at all like the native mythology of Anatolia but typical of material of a foreign origin. A comparison of the Illuyanka myth with that of Kumarbi stresses the difference. The Kingship in Heaven text and the Song of Ullikummi are in fact Hurrian myths, either translated straight into Hittite or freely adapted. An analysis of the divine names which occur in them reveals the influence of the Hurrians and peoples located further to the east: thus 'Kumarbi of Urkish' is pure Hurrian, while Alalu, Anu, and Ea are Babylonian gods. To clinch the matter, fragments of a Hurrian version of the myths have been found at Hattusas. There are embarrassing gaps in our knowledge of the Hurrians, but of one thing, the great impact they had on their neighbours in the western part of the ancient Near East, we can be most certain. It comes as a shock when one realizes for the first time that the gods and goddesses depicted in the relief sculpture of the main gallery at the sanctuary of Yazilikaya are members of the Hurrian and not of the native Hittite

pantheon.[41] A prayer addressed by Queen Puduhepa to the Sun-
goddess of Arinna shows how far the identification of pairs of Hittite
and Hurrian deities progressed: O Sun-goddess of Arinna, queen of
all the countries! In the Hatti country thou bearest the name of the
Sun-goddess of Arinna; but in the land which thou madest the cedar
land thou bearest the name Hebat.[42] Puduhepa herself was a daughter
of a priest from Kummanni, a great cult centre of Hebat in Cilicia, and
her name indicates her devotion to this Hurrian goddess.[43] It is likely,
moreover, that the Hurrians did more than simply influence the
literature and religion of the Hittites, for there is a considerable body
of evidence to make the theory that the Hittite throne was occupied
by a Hurrian dynasty which began with Tudhaliyas II very attractive.[44]
The Hurrians appear to have had so profound an effect on the Hittites
that one scholar feels that we can speak of a culture formed by a blend
of Hurrian and Hittite elements second only to the fusion of Sumerians
and Semites that produced Mesopotamian civilization. The Hurrians
were active from shortly after 2500 B.C. to the early centuries of the first
millennium B.C., and their activities covered an area stretching from
Sumer to the Mediterranean, and from Anatolia to the borders of Egypt.
The Hurrians were both originators and middlemen: from a very early
date they were exposed to the influence of Mesopotamia, and in religion,
law, literature, and art they owed an immense debt to the people of
that country; spreading westwards, they contributed much to the
development of the peoples there as they handed on some of the distinct
features of their own civilization and transmitted others which they
themselves had acquired away in the east.[45] A study of personal names
reveals that a good part, perhaps as much as half, of the population of
Ugarit was Hurrian or Mitannian.[46] It is the presence of such a sizeable
contingent of Hurrians at Ugarit which causes me to claim that, if we
allow our references to Phoenician influence any weight, we ought to
take the Kumarbi and Ullikummi myths into consideration when we
talk about Pherecydes and the Near East. It has already been suggested,
although with great reserve, that we may possess a Ugaritic edition of
the Kingship in Heaven text with El and Baal replacing Kumarbi and
the Storm-god as the main characters.[47] Whether or not the suggestion
turns out to be justified does not matter to us as much as the fact that
the scholar responsible for it sees nothing improbable in such an argument. It is exactly what we may expect if we take into account the
Hurrian group present in the population of Ugarit; it also makes it
easier for us to understand the somewhat ambiguous position in the

Ugaritic pantheon occupied by the god El. As for the Song of Ullikummi, I have pointed out above (p. 10) that Mount Hazzi stands beside the Orontes river. The mountain, the highest in this part of Syria, is some twenty-five to thirty miles distant from Ugarit further down the coast to the south, and was visible from the town.

Our texts from Ugarit and Hattusas and Philo of Byblos, therefore, are all relevant to the interpretation of Pherecydes. Although there is much doubt as to the events enumerated by Pherecydes and the way in which they were arranged, we do learn from Damascius that the mythographer stated that Chronos ('Time') fashioned from his own seed fire, wind, and water, and that from these, when distributed in five recesses, there arose many other offspring of gods, what is termed the five-recess generation.[48] Kirk sees a parallel to Chronos' use of his own seed as a creative force in the story of Typhon's birth recorded by the B-scholion on Iliad ii, 783. We have had occasion to refer to this tradition earlier (p. 12), when, comparing it with the story of the origin of Ullikummi, we noted the correspondence between parents, Kronos and Kumarbi, and the method of procreation. We have now added another parallel, this time one taken from Pherecydes. West has also compared the story of the birth of Orion, who was reputed to have been born when Hyrieus buried in the earth an ox-hide impregnated by Zeus, Poseidon, and Hermes. One of the sources mentioning the tradition is Nonnus' Dionysiaca (xiii, 98–103). Another reference in Nonnus suggests the Near Eastern origin of the idea, since it takes us to Cyprus and so halfway to the Orient. According to Nonnus (v, 611–5; xiv, 193–202; and xxxii, 71–2), Zeus, hot with passion, once pursued his daughter Aphrodite, but she escaped and Zeus' seed was scattered on the ground. The result of this union between Zeus and the earth was the birth of a peculiar species of Cypriot centaurs equipped with horns.

The five recesses mentioned by Damascius have caused difficulty, for their number seems to clash with the Suda entry on Pherecydes where his book is called 'Seven Recesses'. West is ready to eliminate the problem by emending the Suda reference to read 'Five Recesses'. But Kirk compared the Babylonian myth entitled Descent of Ishtar to the Nether World, in which the goddess has to pass through a series of seven gates in penetrating down into the underworld.[49] Although reluctant to have Pherecydes influenced by traditions emanating from the Near East, even Kirk admits the possibility of a link between the seven recesses of Pherecydes and the seven regions of the Babylonian underworld. The texts from Ugarit, however, offer a more convincing analogy, for in the Baal poem the goddess Anat pays a visit to El who is said to reply to her 'in the seven chambers, inside the eight enclosures'.[50] The number of chambers here suggests that Kirk was correct both in accepting a total of seven recesses and in allowing for the influence of non-Greek material. It seems from the Ugaritic texts that the abode of El was associated with subterranean waters and a mountain. The second detail fits in neatly with Hera burying beneath Arimon of Cilicia the two eggs which Kronos had smeared with semen. Pope may well be right in locating El's home at the modern Khirbet Afqa where the majestic sight of a river issuing from a cavern backed by towering cliffs and then falling down into a deep gorge fulfils all the requirements of the texts.[51] Before leaving the Ugaritic texts we should note that Pherecydes' Ophioneus is not unlike Baal's adversary, the sea-god Yam, and that both the Baal poem and the book by Pherecydes fell of the construction of a palace for the young king of the gods.

The texts from Ugarit refer to El as 'father of the gods' and 'father of mankind', and in the myth which describes how the gods Shachar and Shalim, dawn and dusk, were born, it is El who is their father.[52] Otherwise we know nothing about El as a god of creation. Philo is more informative since he offers us a cosmogony, an account of the origin of certain gods connected with the development of civilized life, and the story of the generations of the gods and their conflicts. One detail from his cosmogony finds an echo in Pherecydes who is reported as saying that Zeus changed into Eros when about to act as creator. Philo claims that Pothos was the beginning of the creation of all things.[53] Apart from scrappy mentions of Ophioneus, we can only guess as to what Pherecydes might have said about the struggle for supremacy in heaven, and there is nothing to set beside the long account given by Philo. If I continue by discussing this, a fundamental difference between the various texts we have so far surveyed and Hesiod's Theogony will become apparent, and it is this difference which will bring us to our second collection of texts, the Babylonian material.

Philo posits four generations of the gods, those of Hypsistos (Eliun), Ouranos, Kronos (El), and Zeus (Demarus). Thus, like the Kumarbi myth, he provides 'Heaven' with a predecessor.[54] The first generation comprised Hypsistos and Beruth, and the second Ouranos and Ge. Ouranos took over control from his father when Hypsistos was killed in an encounter with wild beasts. This strange detail seems to be part of the local Adonis tradition and goes with Philo's earlier statement that Hypsistos and Beruth dwelt about Byblos. Ouranos and Ge had four sons, Kronos, Baitylos, Dagon, and Atlas. Ouranos' abominable conduct towards his consort and his desire to kill their offspring led to a struggle between Kronos and his father. Kronos was victorious in battle and replaced Ouranos, who went off into exile. This, however, is to be no simple story as it is in the Theogony, where Kronos castrates his father and the whole matter is ended. Philo's story does include the castration of Ouranos by Kronos, but this took place only in the thirty-second year of Kronos' reign. Then, we read, Kronos ambushed Ouranos and severed his sexual organs, the blood from which mingled with the water of neighbouring springs and rivers. But the attack occurred inland, and in Philo's own time the place was known. Again one thinks of the Adonis story rather than Hesiod's poem.

But other details recounted by Philo tie in with the texts we have been examining. At an early stage in the conflict Kronos, prompted by his daughter Athene and his scribe Hermes, prepared a sickle and spear of iron. No mention, however, is made of these weapons being used when Kronos and his allies expelled Ouranos. In the battle a concubine of Ouranos was captured and presented as a wife to Dagon. She was already pregnant and shortly gave birth to Demarus, who thus qualifies as the son of both Ouranos and Dagon. The impregnation of Kumarbi when he swallowed the genitals of Anu and the subsequent birth of the Storm-god are an obvious parallel. In spite of his defeat in battle Ouranos was far from being finished, and Kronos hardly made things easy for himself. Suspecting his brother Atlas, Kronos buried him beneath the ground. The incident recalls Hesiod's description of how Ouranos treated his children and not his story of Kronos. Hesiod does not make it clear whether Kronos released his relatives after the overthrow of Ouranos, but later he refers to Zeus setting free the Cyclopes and the Centomani (verses 501–2 and 617–26). Neither the Cyclopes nor the Centomani include Atlas, and Philo's list of the crimes of Kronos – the burying of Atlas, the slaughter of a son named Sadidos, and the beheading of a daughter – appears to owe nothing to the Theogony. It is significant that there is no suggestion that Kronos consumed his own children. But now Ouranos launched fresh assaults against Kronos. First he sent his daughter Astarte with her sisters Rhea and Dione to destroy Kronos by stealth. The Phoenicians, Philo is to inform us later, identified Astarte with Aphrodite, so that here, as in the Theogony, we have Aphrodite made the daughter of Ouranos (pp. 5–6). The attempt to unseat Kronos failed, for the god captured

the goddesses and made them his wives. A second attack, headed by
Heimarmene and Hora, likewise came to nothing when Kronos won
his opponents over to his own side. Then Philo interrupts his recital of
the war between the gods in order to list the birth of a number of children. But the war breaks out again, and Ouranos, allying himself to
Demarus, marched against Pontos. The alliance of Ouranos and
Demarus is reminiscent of the co-operation of Anu and the Storm-god
against Kumarbi. Demarus attacked Pontos but was defeated, while
Ouranos was ambushed by Kronos with a result we have already seen.
Baal, the son of Dagon, is the Ugaritic counterpart of Philo's Demarus,
also a son of Dagon, and the struggle of Baal against the sea-god Yam,
the son of El, matches the battle between Demarus and Pontos. Also
comparable is the clash between Dionysos and Poseidon because of
their simultaneous passion for Beroe, the eponymous heroine of Beirut,
in the forty-third book of the Dionysiaca.[55] The rest of Philo's story can
be told quickly: Kronos set up Astarte, Zeus-Demarus, and Adodos
(i.e. Hadad) as rulers over the earth, and different offices were allocated
to other gods. Kronos gave his daughter Athene the kingdom of Attica,
the goddess Baaltis the city of Byblos, Poseidon Beirut, and Taautos
all Egypt.

The really remarkable thing in this story of the gods is the insignifi-
cance of Zeus. The privileges and even the children of Zeus are
transferred to Kronos. As one scholar has remarked, Kronos replaces
Zeus as the *ordinator rerum*.[56] It is true that in the end Zeus is set up as
ruler, but it is only with the approval of Kronos, who goes on to dis-
tribute cities and countries to the gods. The only part played in the
war by Zeus is an ignominious one when, in the guise of Demarus, he
is routed by Pontos. It is Kronos, furthermore, who acquires wives and
wins the support of forces sent to oppose him by Ouranos. It is the
children of Kronos – nine by Astarte, seven by Rhea, an unspecified
number of daughters by Dione, and three more sons, another Kronos,
Zeus Belos, and Apollo – whose birth causes Philo to turn aside from
the war for a moment. Demarus has to be content with being made the
father of Heracles alone. All this contrasts violently with the picture
we have by the end of the Theogony where Zeus reigns supreme,
marries a number of females by whom he has offspring, and sets the
world in its due order.

Philo illustrates this fundamental difference best, but it can also be
clearly seen in the other texts we have had to consider in this chapter
under the heading of the Hittite material. When it comes to the status

of El in the texts from Ugarit, opinions are sharply divided: some argue for the supremacy of El, but the evidence of the texts themselves seems rather to support the view that El's power is more nominal than real and that it is Baal in fact who is in control of the heavens. Yet the position is confused, for decisions have to be referred to El, so that, even if El has surrendered much of his authority to the young god, Baal is still not supreme to the extent that Zeus undoubtedly is in the Theogony. The Storm-god Teshub is more like Baal than Zeus, for he in both the Kumarbi and Ullikummi myths has yet to attain the dignity of Zeus in the Theogony. One indication of the relative weakness of both Baal and Teshub is the fact that, in addition to winning victory, they also suffer defeat. Often the young god depends upon the help of a powerful ally. Thus Ea has to cripple Ullikummi for Teshub, while in the Baal epic the goddess Anat runs through an impressive list of the enemies of Baal whose defeat she has accomplished.[57] The Storm-god in both versions of the Illuyanka myth and the Song of Ullikummi triumphs after having first experienced defeat. In the same way Apollodorus describes how Zeus was temporarily worsted by Typhon when the dragon robbed Zeus of his sinews. The fact that Apollodorus includes such an episode confirms that the mythographer handles material of a considerable age. As far as we are able to tell, things do not go smoothly for the Storm-god in the Kingship in Heaven text. The so-called KAL text, which may be a separate myth or merely another part of the Kumarbi cycle, reveals that Teshub was not always successful in clinging to his position as king, but was forcibly dispossessed and made to relinquish his throne.[58] The fragmentary nature of this text means that it is impossible to follow the development of its plot in detail, but what can be established shows that the Storm-god was ousted by a god whose name is represented by the word sign KAL. It is likely that Ea was responsible for appointing KAL king. But the deeds of KAL were so arbitrary that they provoked the wrath of Ea, who was obliged to take measures against him. At the end of the text Teshub appears to have been restored to his throne and KAL to have been punished by mutilation.

It is not enough to compare the story told by two or more myths, for of equal importance is their authors' attitude of mind. When we compare the steps by which they climbed to a position of supreme authority, Teshub proves to be no real equivalent of Hesiod's Zeus, and so the religious outlook of the Hittite texts differs from that of the Theogony. Hesiod presents us with a very different picture of the king of the gods, for his Zeus is invincible on the battlefield and wins a resounding victory, unsullied by any defeat, over both the Titans and Typhoeus. When the contents of the Kumarbi and Ullikummi myths and the Theogony were compared, I argued that it is easy to make too much of the few parallels which link the Hittite and Greek texts. This conclusion I repeat with added emphasis now that we have seen that Philo's Zeus-Demarus is subordinate to Kronos, and that Teshub can be stripped of his power. But where are we to go next? We must, I think, first look at the battles fought by Zeus in the Theogony to see if the god is indeed invincible. Then, if we find this to be true, we must consider the one creation epic from the Near East whose hero is a god incapable of suffering defeat, and re-examine a theory originally advanced before the Kingship in Heaven text and the Song of Ullikummi were well known, and a theory, moreover, which in recent years has not received the attention it merits, because we have been preoccupied with texts mistakenly thought to be closer in date to Hesiod. By turning now to Enuma Elish and other Babylonian poems I hope to be able both to reach some positive conclusions and to supplement what has already been said in this chapter about the periods of time at which ideas and traditions were transmitted from the Near East to the Greeks.

Chapter II

THE THEOGONY AND THE BABYLONIAN MATERIAL

ZEUS has three crises to face in the second half of the Theogony. The last of these comes towards the end of the poem when the god has to swallow his first wife Metis to prevent her giving birth to a son who could replace his father as king of gods and men; Gaia and Ouranos were now on the side of the established power, and, by taking their advice, Zeus was able to hold on to his throne (verses 888–900).[1] Zeus had already undertaken two wars, the first against the Titans in order to gain supremacy, and the other with Typhoeus in order to maintain his authority (verses 617 ff. and 820 ff.). The second was won by Zeus without any kind of assistance; it ended with the origin of the winds other than the South, North, and West Winds, produced earlier in the Theogony (verses 378–80). Typhoeus had a hundred snake-heads, each possessing a voice capable of a great variety of sounds (verses 824–35). The closing description of the power of the winds to wreck men at sea and to devastate the fields is clearly intended to echo the description of the dragon's voices (cf. ἄλλοτε in verses 830 etc., and 872, 875, and 878), the link being strengthened by the meaning of the name Typhoeus and the reading ἄνεμον in verse 307. Hesiod's account of this battle, therefore, would seem to fall into three sections, first the birth and physical appearance of Typhoeus, then the actual conflict between god and monster, and finally the origin of the winds from the defeated Typhoeus (verses 820–35, 836–68, and 869–80).[2] The third part, where the varying damage liable to be caused by the adverse winds matches the different voices of Typhoeus, is designed to recall the first.

Things are not so easy for Zeus in the war against the Titans: Zeus has to follow the advice of Gaia (verse 626) and call in the help of the Centomani. The Titanomachia is preceded by the story of Prometheus and a brief mention of the other sons of Iapetos. These provide us with examples of those who challenged the omniscience of Zeus, and, like the Titans, suffered accordingly. The Titanomachia itself opens with a description of the Centomani shut away beneath the earth, an experience they did not find to their liking. Next we are told that Zeus and his brothers and sisters set them free; in doing this, they were carrying out the instructions of Gaia, who had informed the gods that they would win their struggle against the Titans with the help of the Centomani. Up to that time the war between the contending factions had been dragging on for ten full years and had proved indecisive. The Centomani were first restored with nectar and ambrosia, and then Zeus addressed them. The god urged the three Centomani to support him against his enemies, reminding them of their release, and Kottos in reply pledged their assistance (verses 644–53 and 655–63). These speeches call to mind the appeal which Gaia made to her offspring before Ouranos was deposed and the answer given her by her son Kronos (verses 164 ff.). Now that Zeus and his fellows had the support of such powerful allies the battle was rejoined with a fresh enthusiasm. The fact that a second verse 'and those whom Zeus brought up to the light from Erebos beneath the earth' (verse 669) is added to the formulaic line 'the Titan gods and those born of Kronos' (verses 630, 648, and 668; cf. also verses 625, 634, 644, and 660) marks the introduction of a new element into the battle. The struggle culminated in victory for the forces of Zeus, thanks to the efforts of the god himself (verses 687–712), assisted by the Centomani (verses 713 ff.). The latter finally overcame the Titans, who were compelled to take the place of the Centomani and became prisoners beneath the earth.

Passages of direct speech form the climax of this story as they do in other episodes from the Theogony. The beginning and end of the Titanomachia, again in a manner characteristic of Hesiod, are distinguished by a repetition of motif, for the Centomani undergo a complete reversal of fortune, becoming warders where before they had been inmates of the prison (cf. verses 620 and 717, 618 and 718, and 619 and 719). Just as the release of the Centomani was anticipated before the list of the sons of Iapetos (verses 501–6), so at this point Hesiod begins to foreshadow the following description of Tartarus. Schematically the Titanomachia may be divided into the following parts: the release of the Centomani by Zeus (verses 617–28); the failure of Zeus to defeat the Titans (verses 629–42); the speeches of Zeus and Kottos as a climax (verses 643–65); the renewal of battle (verses 665–86); and the final defeat and imprisonment of the Titans (verses 713–35).[3]

From my scheme I have deliberately omitted one passage of considerable length, the description of Zeus in action at the crucial moment when victory is ensured (verses 687–712). Although critical opinion has not been unanimous, several editors of the Theogony have expressed strong doubts as to the authenticity of these verses. Typical were the remarks of Paul Mazon, who, in view of verse 719 (νικήσαντες χερσίν), felt that it was the Centomani who were the victors and that Zeus and his thunderbolts must reflect another tradition.[4] Yet he was prepared to admit on the evidence of verses 504 ff. that Hesiod knew the alternative form of the legend. Was Hesiod responsible for conflating the two traditions to produce the Titanomachia as we have it? Mazon's answer was a negative one. If Zeus was unable to defeat the Titans for a period of ten years, it was because he did not as yet possess his thunderbolts. The Titanomachia, however, says nothing about these weapons being handed over to Zeus. Our text, furthermore, seemed to Mazon to contradict itself badly, for in verse 711 the battle appears to have taken a decisive turn in favour of Zeus, but the Centomani are still having to put up a furious fight two verses later. Mazon would have us believe that such a contradiction is too gross to be allowed to the original poet of the Theogony. But this final objection surely carries little weight: the last war showed time and time again that 'mopping-up' operations can be horribly bloody, and it is mopping-up operations, I suggest, that are being described here, as the war with the Titans draws to its close.

Mazon was right to refer to the earlier passage, where it is said that Zeus released his father's brothers, and that they, out of gratitude for this act of kindness, gave thunder, lightning, and the thunderbolt to their benefactor (verses 501–5). According to verse 141 of the Theogony, the Cyclopes gave thunder to Zeus and fashioned the thunderbolt (cf. verse 504). The birth of the Cyclopes in the Theogony is followed immediately by that of the Centomani (verses 147 ff.), and the two sets of three brothers are not unlike in both strength and disposition. It is the Centomani who are set free at the beginning of the Titanomachia. Although Hesiod does not name their father, the Cyclopes must be the sons of Ouranos. More difficult is the identity of the father – Ouranos (cf. verses 156–8) or Kronos? – mentioned in verses 502 and 617. The same story as recounted by Apollodorus, although much shorter, makes better sense, and I am prepared to accept his interpretation of Hesiod. Both the Centomani and the Cyclopes are made the offspring of Heaven and Earth (1, 1, 1 ff.), and both are hurled into Tartarus by their father. After the overthrow of Ouranos, the prisoners were released and then shut away again, this time by Kronos. Told by Earth that victory was his if he had as allies those in

Tartarus, Zeus set them free, and he and his brothers, Pluto and
Poseidon, received from the Cyclopes their special accoutrements. The
defeated Titans were imprisoned in Tartarus, and the Centomani were
appointed their guards. Hesiod associates the Cyclopes specifically with
thunder and lightning in verse 141 because this association explains
their names of Brontes, Steropes, and Arges. The Cyclopes (verses
501 ff.) and the Centomani (verses 617 ff.) both owe their release from
prison to Zeus, and each group of gods helps Zeus to final victory in its
own way, the Cyclopes by supplying weapons and the Centomani by
service on the battlefield. It is only when we reach verse 504 that we
realize that the father's brothers of verse 501 are the Cyclopes, and
not the Centomani or the Cyclopes and the Centomani. The Cyclopes
and the Centomani are equally in our minds both when we come to
the beginning of the Titanomachia and also as we read through the
Titanomachia.

In the *prooemium* of the Theogony Zeus is said to rule in heaven, alone
possessing thunder and lightning, having subdued his father Kronos by
his might (verses 71–3). Throughout verses 687–712 Zeus is displayed
using these very weapons, and we see how they provide Zeus with the
tools which he needs to accomplish the downfall of his enemies. There
is no inconsistency, as Mazon realized, between Zeus' ten years of
failure and his ultimate triumph over the Titans. But why does Hesiod
not describe Zeus receiving his weapons from the Cyclopes in the
Titanomachia? It is simply because his audience already knows from
verses 501–5 how this came about. To spin out the story of the release
of the prisoners and its consequences any further would only cause the
pace of the action in the Titanomachia to slacken. As it stands, Hesiod's
narrative is wonderfully dramatic. How much more effective it is to see
Zeus using, rather than merely accepting, his new armoury! The
account of the war by Apollodorus, for all its brevity, is comprehensive
and logical. Yet no one could call this an exciting story, however well
it satisfies the demands of a handbook of mythology; too much is
included, and all is too condensed for any of it to arouse our emotions.
Hesiod on the other hand was a poet, and a poet, moreover, whose
purpose it was to communicate to others his burning passion for Zeus.
It was essential that he should select and arrange his material, and this
is exactly what he does with conspicuous success in the Titanomachia.
To confirm the authenticity of verses 687–712, there is the evidence of
verbal repetition which is exploited in order to bind tightly together
these lines and the rest of the story of the war (cf. verses 629, 636, 663,

and 712; 649–50, 677–8, and 688–9; 675, 692, and 715; 678–9 and 693–6; 686 and 705; and 681–3 and 709–10).

In the Titanomachia Zeus stands in need of the help of the Centomani. Homer preserves a tradition which shows that Zeus on at least one later occasion found himself in a desperate plight from which he was saved by the intervention of one of the Centomani. Achilles can remind his mother Thetis of her claim that she alone among the gods rescued Zeus from disaster when Hera, Poseidon, and Athene had wanted to imprison him. Thetis set Zeus free from his bonds, having summoned to Olympus the hundred-handed Briareos, whose arrival was enough to inspire panic in the ranks of the enemies of Zeus (Iliad i, 396–406). There is no reason to suppose that Briareos came equipped with anything beyond his own massive strength (verse 404), and there is certainly no suggestion of special weapons of any kind. But two of the Near Eastern texts which were discussed in chapter one include such an idea. It will be remembered how, in the Song of Ullikummi, the strength of Teshub's rival was undermined when the cutting tool with which Heaven and Earth had originally been separated was produced (pp. 7–8). In the Titanomachia the noise and tumult of the conflict is compared to that to be heard if Gaia and Ouranos came together (verses 702–4), a curious reversal of the situation mentioned to the god Ea by Ubelluri. A better parallel, however, is to be found in the Ugaritic myth of Baal, the first part of which tells of the struggle between Baal and Yam, prince of the sea. Baal is hard put to it until a pair of magic maces is provided by the 'double' god Kathir-and-Khasis. The first mace was given the name of Yagrush and was told to crush Yam's shoulders and chest; the other was called Aymurr, and this one had to complete the mission by smashing in Yam's head.[5] With their assistance Baal vanquished his adversary. In this story, then, the young god depends on special weapons, and they are supplied by an equivalent of the Greek Hephaistos (p. 65). The Cyclopes, of course, often appear as the assistants of Hephaistos.

But we concluded chapter one saying that neither Teshub nor Baal matches the achievements of Hesiod's Zeus. It is true that Metis, if left unchecked, might have produced a successor to Zeus, and that the war against the Titans at first drags on indecisively for ten years, but Zeus weathers both crises without experiencing actual defeat. Hesiod was the master and not the slave of the material at his command, and so he hurries rapidly over any tradition discreditable to Zeus. Thus, when we come to the Titanomachia, we are told virtually nothing about the ten years of stalemate, and the gift of the Cyclopes is ignored. In the exchange between Zeus and Kottos, Hesiod emphasizes the generosity of Zeus in setting the Centomani free, rather than the practical need which dictated his action. The final battle concentrates on the tremendous fury of the onslaught of Zeus, and the Centomani are depicted as effective allies but nothing more than that. To argue that the Titans owe their defeat to the Centomani alone is completely to misunderstand the Theogony. Hesiod's poem is not just the story of the beginnings of the universe and the history of the gods: it is even more a resounding hymn of praise in honour of Zeus, and, unless this is acknowledged, we shall be far from recognizing the message of the Theogony and the intention of its author. Here again the Near East helps us, for the main purpose of the Babylonian Epic of Creation, Enuma Elish, is to celebrate the glory of the young Marduk, and, therefore, its author dwells on the birth of Marduk, his victory over the forces of Tiamat, and the enumeration of the god's names. By the end of Enuma Elish, Marduk has become 'Lord of the Lands' (vii, 136), usurping the title, and therefore the power, of Enlil, the former head of the Babylonian pantheon, while Ea is moved to confer his own name on so magnificent a son. To call the author of Enuma Elish an enthusiast for Marduk is to understate the case, and Zeus in the Theogony and Marduk in Enuma Elish are the two gods, above all others, to be compared.

I am not the first to compare Zeus and Marduk in the Greek and Babylonian poems. In an essay written in 1941 but published in 1950 after his death, Cornford sought to justify the retention of suspect passages in the Theogony, such as the Typhoeus episode, by showing how they formed part of the basic type of creation myth. He drew his evidence in the main from the Genesis story of creation and Enuma Elish.[6] He later elaborated his arguments and examined in greater detail the ritual background of the Babylonian text. Although Cornford's views on the relationship between myth and ritual are highly questionable (pp. 76–7), the conclusions which he reached are worth quoting in their entirety: 'In spite of discrepancies, it is perhaps sufficiently clear that Hesiod's cosmogonical myth is derived ultimately from the Babylonian. The discrepancies are less striking than the coincidences, and less than we might expect when we consider that the story reached Hesiod in fragments detached from the ritual which explained it and gave it coherence'.[7] To this E. R. Dodds added a footnote in which he referred to the publication of the Kumarbi material, stating that the new evidence greatly strengthened Cornford's theory.

⸓ This it certainly does, but new evidence can have its disadvantages: in this case it has had the unfortunate effect of diverting attention away from Enuma Elish, and it has caused us to concentrate too much on one part only of our total evidence. There has been an obvious reason why this should be so. The tablets from Hattusas date from between 1400 to 1200 B.C., while the Theogony would seem to have been composed within a few years of 700 B.C. It has generally been considered that Enuma Elish goes back to the Old Babylonian period, and, to be precise, to the reign of King Hammurabi of Babylon in the eighteenth century B.C. So early a date for the original composition of Enuma Elish does not necessarily mean that it had less influence on the Theogony, for we possess copies of the poem which are later in date than Hesiod himself. Yet one has tended to think of an eighteenth-century Enuma Elish as the archetype from which both the Kumarbi myth and the Theogony are ultimately derived.[8] It is tempting to conclude that the Kumarbi myth and the Theogony are correspondingly closer in contents as they are closer in date. Orientalists, however, are in the process of modifying their opinion of the date of Enuma Elish. Our earliest fragments of the epic cannot be dated with precision, but they fall between the reign of Tiglath-pileser I (*c.* 1100 B.C.) and the Late Assyrian period. A fresh assessment of the position of Marduk among the gods of Mesopotamia suggests that his rise to supremacy was a relatively late development. In terms of chronology, Enuma Elish now seems to stand between the Hattusas tablets and the Theogony, a fact which explains why the Kingship in Heaven text and the Song of Ullikummi feature Ea and Enlil, but appear to mention Marduk only as one of the gods with whom Kumarbi was impregnated after he had swallowed the genitals of Anu (p. 2). Even here Marduk may not be meant, for the actual name Marduk does not appear and this may be a separate deity who was identified with Marduk only at a later date.[9] Its revised date precludes any possibility of Enuma Elish having influenced the Mycenaean Greeks. But this and related matters I propose to leave on one side for the present, while we acquire a clearer picture of the contents of the Babylonian Epic of Creation.

It is a great relief to note that there are very few gaps in our text of Enuma Elish. Work carried out in the last few years means that we can now follow the course taken by events in the fifth tablet of the poem, while tablets recovered from Sultantepe supplement the text in a

number of places. Such developments make it imperative that we
re-examine Enuma Elish to see whether it parallels the story told in
the Theogony more consistently than any of the other texts which we
have so far analysed. The complete poem covers seven tablets, and the
first begins with the statement that, before heaven and earth existed,
the gods were created within Apsu and Tiamat, two kinds of primeval
water mingled to form a single body.[10] Next there came into existence
two pairs of deities, Lahmu and Lahamu, and Anshar and Kishar; the
second pair gave birth to a son named Anu, and then Anu begot Ea,
here called Nudimmud, a god 'broad of understanding, wise, mighty
in strength, much stronger than his grandfather, Anshar' (i, 18–9).
The gods behaved so uproariously that their high spirits upset Tiamat
and disturbed Apsu, who, accompanied by his vizier Mummu, went
to discuss the situation with Tiamat. She, however, was horrified by
Apsu's proposal to destroy what they themselves had brought forth, all
for the sake of peace and quiet. Although Tiamat recommended
patience, Apsu was egged on by Mummu. But the plot was discovered,
and at this moment of crisis Ea displayed his wisdom by casting a spell
which plunged Apsu into a deep sleep. This gave him the opportunity
to strip Apsu of his royal insignia and to appropriate his power; Apsu
was slain and Mummu locked away. In this incident the author of
Enuma Elish betrays an interest in aetiology, for he has thus explained
why Ea is able to occupy the Apsu and how the god made the wisdom
of Mummu his own. The significance of Mummu is suggested by
Damascius, who, following the peripatetic philosopher Eudemus of
Rhodes, says that he conceives Moymis (Mummu) to be τὸν νοητὸν
κόσμον.[11] By subduing Mummu, therefore, Ea seems to have done much
the same thing as Zeus did when he swallowed Metis. Ea's trick calls
to mind the way in which Hera persuades Hypnos to lull Zeus to sleep
in the *Dios Apate* (Iliad xiv, 231 ff.), while the disagreement between
Apsu and Tiamat suggests the brief reference to the quarrel between
Okeanos and Mother Tethys in the same part of the Iliad (verses 200 ff.)
    The next event to be recorded is the birth in the Apsu of Marduk, the
son of Ea and his wife Damkina. There follows an impressive description of Marduk where we read of his father's pleasure at such a son,
not the least of whose attributes are four eyes and four ears! Indeed
Marduk was endowed with an extraordinary godhead, and this was
just as well, for Tiamat was disturbed again and was being pressed to
avenge her husband Apsu. This time she was moved to take action and
formed an opposition party, giving birth to eleven monsters which

became part of her army, and investing the god Kingu with supreme power. Tiamat made Kingu her only consort and handed over to him the Tablet of Destinies. It is not easy trying to identify the various gods who attached themselves to the side of Tiamat, but Kingu, who is introduced so abruptly into the narrative, was apparently one of Tiamat's sons (i, 146). When at the beginning of the second tablet he informs his grandfather Anshar of the impending danger, Ea can say that 'all the gods went over to her; even those whom ye have created march at her side' (ii, 13–4). From Marduk's reply to Tiamat before they fight their duel, it would seem, moreover, that the sons have rebelled and are attacking their fathers (iv, 79). One must conclude that Tiamat was able to command wide support and that her allies were not restricted to her own immediate offspring. By the close of tablet one the scene has been set, and we wait impatiently for the inevitable trial of strength between Tiamat and Marduk.

In fact, we have still to wait for some time. In the second tablet Ea, unnerved by Tiamat's preparations, consults Anshar; he was advised to give the enemy the same sort of treatment he had once meted out to Apsu. Ea's reply is lost, but later Anshar says that Ea was afraid and turned back (iii, 54). When the text commences again, Anshar has turned to Anu, whom he despatches in an attempt to pacify Tiamat. But Anu could not face her, and this second failure left the gods silent and despondent. Ea, however, now interviewed Marduk privately, and suggested that he present himself to Anshar, ready for battle. Marduk restored heart to Anshar and guaranteed victory, but in return he demanded that the gods recognize his supremacy; for the future it was to be Marduk's word which determined the Fates and no one was to challenge it. The third tablet opens with Anshar despatching his vizier to report the news to Lahmu and Lahamu and to collect the gods together. This and the next tablet continue the story by telling how Marduk's proposal was put to the gods, who agreed and granted him supreme power. The fact that Marduk could perform a miracle by making a constellation vanish and then reappear at his command proved the reality of his power.

Marduk next equipped himself with a formidable array of weapons, a bow, a club, lightning, and a net with which to ensnare his foe. Aided already by the south wind, north wind, east wind, and the west wind, the young god also created seven winds 'to trouble Tiamat within' (iv, 48). He 'raised the rain flood, his mighty weapon' (iv, 49),

4

and mounted his storm-chariot, drawn by a team of four, the Destructive, the Pitiless, the Trampler, and the Flier. 'On his right he placed fierce battle and resistance, on his left strife that overthrows the proud' (iv, 55–6).[12] Even so, Marduk can only be victorious after an initial rebuff, for, when Marduk approached Tiamat and surveyed his opponent, both he and his followers were thrown into disorder.[13] Tiamat and Marduk exchanged words which ended in a challenge to single combat. Marduk spread out his net and enmeshed Tiamat, while the winds kept Tiamat's mouth propped open and her body distended; thereupon Marduk administered the killing blow, shooting an arrow into her middle. Tiamat's supporters, including the monsters and Kingu, were soon rounded up and imprisoned. Finally, Marduk turned back to the body of Tiamat and used his club to split her skull; then he divided her body into two parts to create heaven and earth, and 'Anu, Enlil, and Ea he then caused to inhabit their residences' (iv, 146), although the last named, we remember, has been occupying the Apsu for some considerable time.

The first part of tablet five sees Marduk installing the stars, moon, and sun, and arranging that the weather should function and that water, including the Euphrates and Tigris rivers, be available. References to the udder of Tiamat, and, in the next section of the poem, to her tail show that Tiamat, previously depicted as a mass of water in which the gods were born and then in the battle as a monster with a solid body, was also represented as a gigantic animal – actually a goat, according to Lambert. Comparable is Styx, who in the Theogony appears both as a person (verses 383 ff.) and as water (verses 775 ff.). The formation of the universe was completed by Marduk when the god had ensured it was firmly tied together with the cosmic rope. The second and longer part of tablet five starts by describing how Marduk disposed of his trophies and was greeted by the gods, who presented him with gifts and acknowledged his sovereignty. After Marduk had assumed the royal insignia and taken his place on his throne, the gods reaffirmed their loyalty, and their king announced the building of Babylon to serve as a meeting-place for the gods. Questioned by the gods as to their future status, Marduk satisfied them that he would not encroach on any of their privileges and received a last declaration of allegiance. In the sixth tablet we pass on to the creation of mankind. Next Marduk assigned the Anunnaki in equal numbers to heaven and the underworld. To express their gratitude, they proceeded to construct the city of Babylon and Marduk's great temple. There the gods gathered for a banquet and confirmed yet again the supreme authority of Marduk, whose unlimited power was indicated by the recital of his 'fifty' names. The proclamation of these names covers the rest of the sixth tablet and all of tablet seven with the exception of a short epilogue. The nine names conferred on Marduk in tablet six and the forty-two which he receives in the closing tablet provide Enuma Elish with a fitting climax which forcibly hammers home the true purpose of its author, the glorification of the great god of Babylon. We may call Enuma Elish a creation epic, but such a description is hardly adequate and does not give a balanced picture of its contents. It is much better called a hymn to Marduk, and Lambert informs me that in the epilogue to the poem it is indeed termed 'Song of Marduk'. In the same way we fail to appreciate the significance of the Theogony, if we deny that Hesiod himself composed the description of Zeus overwhelming the Titans with his thunderbolts. The Theogony, like Enuma Elish, concentrates on the exploits of the king of the gods, and it is as much a eulogy of the power of Zeus as Hesiod's other poem, the Works and Days.

Irrespective of its date of composition, one would expect the author of Enuma Elish to have taken advantage of traditional material. It is the growth in importance of the god Marduk which offers the main clue to the date of Enuma Elish. Recently a study of a wide range of contemporary material has shown how wrong we are to exaggerate the prominence of Marduk at the time of the First Dynasty of Babylon: the idea that Marduk was the supreme god must be a later development.[14] Lambert believes that this idea developed during the latter part of the Cassite period (*c.* 1500–1200 B.C.), and that it was officially accepted during the reign of Nebuchadnezzar I of the Second Dynasty of Isin in the last quarter of the twelfth century B.C. Lambert, while stressing the dangers of trying to be too precise, argues that the evidence which we have at the moment makes the reign of Nebuchadnezzar I the most likely period when the Babylonian Epic of Creation was composed.[15] What is even more important from our point of view is the fact that it seems impossible for Enuma Elish to have been compiled before that date. Enuma Elish of Middle Babylonian date can, therefore, be cited as further proof to show that the creative impulse was far from being dead in literature produced after the Old Babylonian period.[16]

Ashur, the national god of Assyria, can replace Marduk in Assyrian recensions of Enuma Elish. It is not surprising then that it has been suggested that Marduk is a substitute for the god Enlil in some earlier version of the creation epic. It is true that the author of Enuma Elish is anxious to avoid any reference to Marduk's greatest rival; we must wait until the last line of tablet four before Enlil is even mentioned in the poem. By the end of Enuma Elish Marduk has completely eliminated Enlil, since fifty is the sacred number of Enlil and 'Lord of the Lands' the rival god's title. But the prior existence of a creation epic whose hero was Enlil is just a hypothesis, and there is no scrap of evidence to substantiate it. The long established use of writing throughout the Near East to record literary and religious texts means that the Akkadian specialist has at his disposal some of the raw material from which Enuma Elish was created. Lambert has collected the evidence for Babylonian theogonies, and it is his conclusions which I present here. The major gods of the Babylonian pantheon in the second millennium B.C. were Enlil and Anu, the former in practice being the more powerful. Both were reputed to have been descended from primary forces, Earth in the case of Enlil, and either Nammu, primeval water, or Duri Dari, 'ever and ever', in the case of Anu. The descent of Anu as it is known from incantation texts is the tradition which influenced the sequence of divine kings in the Kumarbi myth, for it makes the pair Alala and Belili the immediate predecessors of Anu and Antum.[17] That force was used to achieve supreme power is another idea which can be traced back to Babylonian sources, but our material is somewhat thin; Enuma Elish itself reveals that Anshar, the father of Anu, was once king of the gods, as Anshar regularly takes charge of the situation and in one line is actually called king of the gods (iv, 83). The theogony with which Enuma Elish opens is an adaptation of the alternative theogonies of Anu, taking the concept of primeval water, although Apsu and Tiamat replace Nammu, from the one tradition represented by an Old Babylonian god list, and the idea of descent through matched pairs (Apsu and Tiamat, Lahmu and Lahamu, Anshar and Kishar) from the incantation texts. At the same time Ea, who is always the father of Marduk and himself traditionally the son of either Nammu or Anu, is introduced into the genealogy, so that the birth of Marduk may be accommodated. All three primary forces of the Babylonians appear in Greek authors: with Duri Dari we seem to have the principle of eternal time, and so a convincing prototype of Pherecydes' Χρόνος; Homer's Okeanos, 'the genesis of the gods' and 'genesis of all' (Iliad xiv, 201 and 246), represents the concept of primeval water, now made a river which surrounds the earth (Iliad xviii, 607–8); in Hesiod's

Theogony Earth is one of the *Urgötter* produced when Chaos came into being (verses 116 ff.).

There is a number of 'loose ends' in Enuma Elish, some of which may be evident from my summary of the contents of the poem, brief though that was. Kingu, for example, appears very suddenly on the scene and contributes nothing to the battle. The verdict of the jury which has him slain in order to provide the blood necessary to create mankind is a strange one. It is difficult, therefore, to resist the conclusion that Kingu was brought into the plot to make Marduk's triumph even more resounding and also to provide the blood of a suitable victim. Although Kingu received the Tablet of Destinies from Tiamat, Marduk could demand that Anshar allow him to determine the Destinies in place of Anshar (iii, 120), and, when in the fifth tablet Marduk disposes of his trophies, he is said to have presented to Anu the Tablet of Destinies, which he had taken away from Kingu (v, 69–70). As Lambert remarks, the author of Enuma Elish does not take the Tablet of Destinies too seriously. But why, then, does he bother with the idea at all? The answer seems to be that the conflict between Marduk and Tiamat is modelled on the earlier tradition of the god Ninurta's struggle with the monstrous Zu bird.[18] In this myth, of which we have a substantial part of the Old Babylonian text, the Tablet of Destinies plays a significant part. The myth tells how the bird-god Zu stole the Tablet from Enlil and thus gained for himself complete authority. Anu, who, as Lambert reminds us, was sometimes identified with Anshar, invited a god to recover the Tablet, but two who were approached – Adad and Shara – both declined; then, at the instigation of Ea and the Mother-goddess, Ninurta (Ningirsu according to the Old Babylonian version found at Susa) was sent to deal with Zu. His first attempt failed when Zu by uttering a spell and raising the Tablet in his hands reduced Ninurta's arrow to its constituent elements. Ninurta, having received more instructions from Ea, resumed the battle, and this time Zu was defeated. Gurney has already said that 'the struggle between Ninurta and Zu is in a sense the prototype of that between Marduk and Tiamat', and the confusion over the Tablet of Destinies in Enuma Elish bears out his claim. Lambert adds that Ninurta is the dragon-slayer *par excellence* in Mesopotamian tradition and wins eleven victories, mostly over monsters. Determined to show that his own god could do just as well, the devotee of Marduk who composed Enuma Elish must include eleven monsters among the retinue of Tiamat. We also know of another myth where a god is matched against a monster, but our text is in a wretched state. This monster is called the *labbu* and that should mean that it is some kind of lion.[19] We read in the text, however, that the monster was a dragon brought forth by the sea and of a colossal size, both suggestive details. As far as we can tell, Tishpak was unwilling or unable to oppose the creature, and another god had to finish it off with the bow. The interesting point in this myth is the fact that its opening lines refer to the cities sighing and the people decreasing in number. The Babylonians knew, therefore, of an occasion when a dragon challenged the authority of the gods at a later stage in the history of the universe than that associated with Marduk's victory over Tiamat, in fact not before but after mankind had been created and cities built. One thinks here of Zeus and Typhoeus in the Theogony, for, if Zeus had not been quick to notice the dragon, the latter would have ruled over mortals and immortals (verses 837–8).

Lambert believes that the catalogue of Marduk's 'fifty' names was a separate work borrowed by the author of Enuma Elish with little or no change. As a result we find references which are inconsistent with what is said elsewhere in the poem. The use of traditional catalogues which do not conform in every detail to the setting in which they have been preserved is something known to every student of Greek epic, the Catalogue of Ships in the second book of the Iliad being the most obvious example. The very first of the many catalogues included in the Theogony reveals that such material need be only partially integrated: to understand the inclusion of Dione in verse 17 we must rely not on the Theogony where she appears otherwise merely as one of the many daughters of Okeanos (verse 353), but on a passage in the Iliad which makes the goddess the mother of Aphrodite (v, 370–1). To remove the roll-call of Marduk's names from the Babylonian poem would destroy its tremendous conclusion. Furthermore, as early as the first tablet, we meet a name of Marduk and an interpretation of that name (i, 101–2).

Enuma Elish opens with a theogony and has nothing comparable to Hesiod's lengthy prelude to the Heliconian Muses. Preambles are not common in Babylonian literature, although the Epic of Gilgamesh and the Myth of Zu are exceptions, as is the Kingship in Heaven text. The generations of the gods comprise Apsu and Tiamat, the two pairs, Lahmu and Lahamu and Anshar and Kishar, Anu, and finally Anu's son Ea. If one examines Hesiod's list of the powers which appear before the union of Gaia and Ouranos, it will be found that they fall into sets of pairs (Gaia and Eros, Erebos and Night, Aither and Hemera) as do the first gods of Enuma Elish.[20] The pairs, however, become a triad when Gaia gives birth to Ouranos, the Mountains, and Pontos (verses 126 ff.). All three children in this last grouping are difficult. The inclusion of Ouranos must imply that Gaia here is not simply the earth but something like the universe, for, while mountains and the sea cover much of the earth's surface, this can scarcely be said of heaven, at least not in the same sense. References in the Theogony show that land and sea formed a natural pair for Hesiod (verses 762, 790, and 972; 964; and 843–5), to which heaven could be added as a third element (verses 427, 678–80, and 847). The list might be extended by the further addition of Tartarus (verses 736–7 and 807–8), of Okeanos and Tartarus (verses 839–41), and of the underworld (verses 847–52), but nowhere by the addition of the Mountains. Outside verse 129, the Mountains are ignored by Hesiod, and we may conclude that they are an artificial creation of the poet, chosen to complete the grouping heaven, land, and sea, and, at the same time, to prevent too glaring a clash with the mother of the triad, Gaia herself. If the Mountains are excluded, we are left with what was originally another pair, Ouranos and Pontos.

Pontos is another problem, this time for two reasons. First, among the offspring of Ouranos and Gaia is included Okeanos (verse 133). It is clear that Pontos and Okeanos are two distinct types of water: Pontos is the sea, while Okeanos, the father of the rivers, is the source of all rivers. Thus in one passage (verses 695–6) Okeanos's streams appear with land and *pontos* to express the totality of earth and water. But Pontos and Okeanos can also serve as alternatives, so that, when two of the short catalogues from the *prooemium* of the Theogony are compared, we find in one Dawn, Sun, and Moon (= heaven), Gaia, Okeanos, and Night (verses 19–20), but in the other Earth, Ouranos, Night, and Pontos (verses 106–7), the second of these lists being directly followed by another mentioning gods, earth, rivers, sea, stars, and heaven (verses 108–10). Secondly, we must ask why Pontos is placed with Ouranos and before Okeanos so early in the development of the cosmos. The importance of Ouranos is obvious: he is the direct opposite of the earth and covers earth completely (verses 126–7), and is soon to join with Gaia in providing the gods with their first king and queen. Pontos can claim no such honour, nor does Pontos in Hesiod seem to be a form of the primeval water.

If it may be assumed that Hesiod was handling traditional material, according to which Sea was descended in the second generation from Earth, we are able to appreciate the position of Pontos in the poet's scheme. A newly identified Babylonian text allows that assumption to be made, for it lists as the first three generations of the gods three pairs, Hain and Earth, Amakandu and Sea, and Lahar and River.[21] Now for the first time we have more to compare than the Babylonian Earth and Hesiod's Gaia, as Sea as the feminine element in the second generation and the corresponding position in the third generation occupied by River throw fresh light on the facts that Pontos is the offspring of Gaia, and that the birth of Pontos precedes that of Okeanos. This text is known from a Late Babylonian tablet on the obverse of which some forty lines, not all complete, are preserved. Although little survives of the reverse, a reference in the colophon supplies a *terminus ante quem* of 614 B.C. for the text, which apparently reflects the local mythology of an obscure city named Dunnu. The text also relates the story of the dynasties of heaven and tells how Amakandu, on the initiative of Earth, married his mother and killed his father Hain. At first this suggests Hesiod's story of the overthrow of Ouranos by Kronos, especially since to marry one's mother and to castrate one's father express the same subconscious desire. But the link with the first deities of the Theogony is even closer: while the Titans freely contract brother-sister marriages – Tethys and Okeanos (verse 337), Theia and Hyperion (verses 371–4), Phoibe and Koios (verse 404), and Rhea and Kronos (verse 453) – it is only Ouranos and Pontos who practise incest to the extent of mating with their own mother, Ouranos to produce a whole horde of children (verses 132 ff.) and Pontos (verse 238) to produce Nereus, Thaumas, Phorkys, Keto, and Eurybie. There is only one other example in the Theogony of a union between mother and her child, namely when the combination of Echidna and Orthos gives birth to the Sphinx and Nemean Lion (verses 326–7), and here the reference to Echidna is not entirely certain.

As Enuma Elish unfolds, we find Apsu, like Ouranos, cast as the wicked parent who plans to destroy his descendants, but Tiamat is opposed to Apsu's schemes and at first remains neutral, whereas Gaia actively encourages her son Kronos. Ea corresponds to Kronos, for both gods are associated with immense cunning and craft; they succeed in thwarting Apsu and Ouranos respectively. Ea, however, proves to be a kind father who welcomes the birth of his son Marduk and does all he can to promote his rise. There is no clash of interests between Ea and Marduk as there is between Kronos and Zeus. It is noticeable that Hesiod concentrates on the story of the birth of Zeus and has nothing to say about either Zeus' part in forcing Kronos to disgorge his offspring or Kronos' activities in the Titanomachia.[22] If Marduk and Zeus were to win all the credit they deserved for their victories, both the forces of Tiamat and the Titans had to be made formidable opponents. The author of Enuma Elish solves the problem, first by making Marduk succeed where other gods had failed, and secondly by making Marduk experience a moment of panic; Hesiod allows for ten years of fighting in which neither side was able to gain the upper hand. Tiamat's band of rebels seems to have included both old and young gods, and there is no clear division between the different generations of the gods. Thus Kingu became the consort of Tiamat, while Anshar organized the forces on the other side. In the same way Zeus could count on the support of some of the older deities, such as the Centomani. Styx also pledged her support and that of her children, Zelos, Nike, Kratos, and Bia, when Zeus had summoned all the immortals to Olympus and guaranteed to safeguard or, if they had none before, to promote the privileges of those who fought with him against the Titans (verses 389 ff.). On this occasion the gods were gathered together in assembly and a formal agreement concluded. The strict legality of Zeus' actions suggests the god as we know him in the Works and Days – Zeus the god who vindicates the just and destroys the unrighteous. In Enuma Elish the rebel gods hold a meeting to prepare for the fight, and Tiamat appoints Kingu to the supreme command. On the other side Marduk is elected leader, and then, after the foe has been crushed, we read on the fifth tablet how the gods declare their allegiance to Marduk twice, the second time, moreover, after Marduk has been asked about their future status and has given a reassuring answer. Tablet six has the gods again acknowledging the supremacy of Marduk's rule.

Among Marduk's most potent forces are the winds: the four main winds were created by Anu at the time of Marduk's birth (i, 105); Marduk himself brought forth another seven before the battle. At an early stage in the Theogony Hesiod describes how Eos and Astraios gave birth to the West, North, and South Winds (verses 378–80); the other winds were produced from the body of the defeated Typhoeus. Tiamat also had valuable allies, the eleven monsters. According to the Theogony, Typhoeus mated with the frightful Echidna (verses 306 ff.), and their offspring consisted of a series of horrible monsters, the hounds Orthos and Kerberos, the Hydra, and the Chimaira. Echidna and Orthos, as we have seen above, produced the Sphinx and the Nemean Lion. But her allies did not save Tiamat, for she herself was slain by

Marduk, while her forces, like Hesiod's Titans, were locked away in prison and bound fast. The defeated monsters appear again in tablet five where lines 73–6 read:

And her eleven creatures, whom Tiamat had created and . . . . .,
whose weapons were broken and whom he had fettered to his foot,
their images he fashioned and placed at the Gate of Apsu,
saying, 'This shall be a token that shall never be forgotten!'[23]

It has been noted that these lines recall an earlier passage (iv, 115–8 and iv, 111), while v, 77–82 recall iv, 133–4, and v, 119–22 and v, 125–8 anticipate vi, 61–6 and vi, 52–4. The use of parallel passages to refer to what has gone before and to what will presently be described is characteristic of Hesiod.

That Enuma Elish is really a hymn to Marduk can be seen if one looks at the closing list of the god's names. This affords an example of a catalogue which even Hesiod in his most ambitious mood would be hard pressed to better. The names and accompanying explanations of them leave us in no doubt as to the range of Marduk's power. If the passage which describes the eighteenth name of Marduk is quoted, we shall acquire a good idea of what this part of Enuma Elish looks like, and we shall also see that Marduk, like Zeus, functions as the god of justice:

Shazu, who knows the hearts of the gods, who sees through the
innermost parts;
from whom the evildoer cannot escape;
the establisher of the assembly of the gods, who gladdens
their hearts;
their wide protection, the subduer of the disobedient;
the administrator of justice, who puts an end to crooked speech;
who in his place discerns falsehood and truth (vii, 35–40).

It is inevitable that we ask if this list of names has any counterpart in the Theogony. Catalogues of names occur throughout Hesiod's poem, and sometimes, as in the names of Marduk, we see elaborate play on their etymology. One example is offered by verses 233–6, where Nereus is described. The first of these verses calls him ἀψευδέα and ἀληθέα. The second epithet is echoed by the οὐδὲ θεμιστέων λήθεται of verses 235–6, while the two adjectives in verse 235 explain his name of Nereus. His daughters, the Nereids, include deities whose names refer to their father's power of prophecy and his concern for justice, most clearly in the case of Nemertes 'who has the mind of her immortal sire' (verse 262) and Themisto (cf. verses 235 and 261).[24] But what do we find towards the close of the Theogony? The answer is a catalogue not of the names of Zeus, but of the wives of Zeus and of the children born as a result of these marriages. This catalogue follows the Typhoeus episode and, more significantly, a passage of five lines where the gods are said to have urged Zeus to become their king and he distributed their honours to them (verses 881–5). Zeus made Metis his first wife and Athene was born. Then Zeus and Themis mated together and had as children the Horai, Eunomia, Dike, Eirene, and the Fates. Eurynome bore the Graces to Zeus; Demeter gave birth to Persephone; Mnemosyne was the mother of the Muses; Apollo and Artemis were born to Zeus and Leto; and Hera, the god's last wife, bore Hebe, Ares, and Eileithyia (verses 886–923). Before our text ends, Zeus also has Hermes by Maia, Dionysos by Semele, and Heracles by Alkmene (verses 938–44). At the end of the Theogony, therefore, instead of an enumeration of the names of the king of the gods, we hear of his marriages and liaisons. But is this so very different, once it is recognized that, like a name, the choice of a particular partner and the children born from that union are designed to express various aspects of the god's power?

Because of the recent article by Landsberger and Kinnier Wilson, we now know much more about the contents of the fifth tablet of Enuma Elish. The cosmogonical description occupies lines 1–66 of the tablet, and is divided into the following sections by the two scholars: Marduk installs the stars (1–10); Marduk installs the moon (11–26); Marduk installs the sun (27–44); Marduk introduces weather phenomena (45–52); the opening of the sources (53–8); and the final locking of the cosmos (59–66). Perhaps the fifth section requires a word of explanation: it tells how Marduk allowed water to trickle from the body of Tiamat. He piled a mountain on her head, letting the Euphrates and Tigris escape through her eyes, and drilled fountains through her dugs to set more water free. If we wish to locate a passage in Hesiod's poem whose contents are comparable, we must turn to verses 337–45, where we have a catalogue of famous rivers, or to verses 371–82, where Theia and Hyperion produce the Sun, Moon, and Eos, and then Eos and Astraios give birth to the stars. Both passages come from the first intermezzo, the part of the Theogony which separates the story of Ouranos from that of his successor Kronos (pp. xii–xiii). The episode which follows the story of the defeat of the Titans and thus occupies the same position in the narrative as the cosmogony of Enuma Elish is Hesiod's description of Tartarus or the second intermezzo.[25] We should expect

to find some coincidence of subject-matter when we compare the f
and the second intermezzo, and this proves to be so, for repeated then
include a description of Night (verses 211 ff. and 744 ff.), her childr
Thanatos and Hypnos (verses 212 and 756 ff.), the Sun (verses 3
and 759–61), Kerberos (verses 310–2 and 769–74), Styx (verses 3(
and 383 ff., and 775 ff.), Iris (verses 266 and 780 ff.), the dangers
a false oath (verses 231–2 and 793 ff.), and the Nereid-type nam
Kymopoleia (verse 819). The description of Tartarus, nevertheles
lacks the long genealogies which fill so much of the first intermezzc
In fact, this is the only extensive extract in the Theogony to offe.
cosmogonical information, uninterrupted by genealogy.

Marduk, as we know the god in Enuma Elish, seems to me to be the
closest equivalent of Hesiod's Zeus. In all fairness I must point out
that Lambert does not believe that Enuma Elish influenced the Theogony. His reason is not related to the analogies between the two poems
which I have attempted to establish, and on these to a large extent
must rest the ultimate judgment as to the soundness of my argument.
His objection is a weighty one and requires careful consideration. It is
based upon the revised dating of Enuma Elish and the fact that he has
shown the poem to be a highly composite work whose author was
certainly not unoriginal. As long as Enuma Elish was thought to have
been composed at the time of the First Dynasty of Babylon, it could
be assumed that it was known for not far short of two thousand years.
It followed that it was *the* Babylonian creation myth and reproduced
the orthodox theology of the inhabitants of Mesopotamia. Enuma
Elish dating from about 1100 B.C. may be the longest and best
preserved creation text to have survived from the Near East, but we
can no longer argue as if it faithfully presents views that were widely
accepted over a very long period of time. Neither of the two short
extracts in Greek which record the Babylonian story of creation
corresponds in every detail with Enuma Elish, although the author of
one, Berossus, was himself a priest of Marduk at Babylon. The other
version does something which the author of Enuma Elish takes pains
to avoid doing: it makes provision in its theogony for Enlil by having
Kissare and Assoros (Kishar and Anshar) produce three sons, Anos,
Illinos, and Aos (Anu, Enlil, and Ea).[26] In tracing the history of
Enuma Elish, Lambert suggests that, while the ideas it expressed made
considerable headway, alternative myths were not suppressed and, even
in Babylon, might be preferred. Once we cease regarding Enuma Elish
as the canonical tradition and we recognize it for what it undoubtedly

is, the work of a man who either inaugurated or followed a new trend, then we may no longer assume that it was well known and accepted to such an extent that its influence spread and was welcome everywhere throughout the Near East. If we appear to be able to identify elements common to Enuma Elish and the Theogony, these may be the result not of the influence of one poem on the other, but rather the result of a common legacy and one which possibly goes as far back as the Neolithic period.

Yet counter arguments are possible. Thus Lambert maintains that Enuma Elish must have been popular in Assyria about the middle of the seventh century B.C., because the library of Ashurbanipal at Nineveh, in addition to texts of the poem itself, has also yielded two commentaries, one on the complete text and the other on the seventh tablet of Enuma Elish. The Assyrians, moreover, had their own version of the poem with Ashur substituted for the Babylonian god Marduk. If Enuma Elish was first composed *c.* 1100 B.C., it could not have been known to the Mycenaean Greeks, and its influence, if any, on the Greeks must date from the period when Greece had recovered from the shock of the Dorian Invasion and contact with the Near East was re-established. Detailed arguments must be reserved until the last chapter of the book, but it may be provisionally suggested that this implies as the earliest possible date for the Greeks to have become acquainted with Enuma Elish some time in the late ninth century B.C. The *floruit* of Hesiod, and here again I can only dogmatically state what will later be argued in detail, was about 730 B.C. Both of these dates bring us close to the heyday of Enuma Elish in Assyria. But it is the discovery of fragments of the text which offers the only certain evidence as to the spread of knowledge of Enuma Elish. Here the Sultantepe finds are significant, for this site is located about twenty miles north of Harran and fifty miles to the east of the Euphrates crossing at Carchemish. It stands, therefore, roughly halfway between Nineveh and the Mediterranean coast and, as Al Mina and Tell Sukas tell us (pp. 121–2), Greek settlers. The Assyrians, moreover, controlled Syria during the second half of the ninth century B.C. and again when, shortly after 750 B.C., Tiglath-pileser III ascended the throne. Also suggestive is the character of the collection of texts from Sultantepe, a small provincial town. There is a considerable variety of texts, some literary and others whose contents are non-literary. The first group includes a complete tablet four and a nearly complete tablet six of Enuma Elish. The texts in the main date from the seventh century B.C.

and appear to represent the library of a certain Qurdi-Nergal. Although Qurdi-Nergal was a priest, there is no reason for us to suppose that his was a temple, rather than a private, collection of tablets.[27]

In my comparison of Enuma Elish and the Theogony I tried to show how the poems share the same spirit in the sense that they both paint the same picture of an all-powerful and just king of the gods. Yet Marduk is an oriental god and can receive the kind of homage which no Greek god pays to one of his fellows, however supreme. After Marduk in Enuma Elish had disposed of his trophies, the gods presented him with gifts and indulged in what a Greek would consider gross adulation :

> Assembled were the Igigi, they prostrated before him altogether,
> as many as they were, the Anunnaki kissed his feet;
> they came in their entirety to pay him reverence, and
> stood before him, did obeisance, saying 'King is he indeed!'
>
> (v, 85–8).[28]

In the Iliad the Olympians may rise in respect when Zeus or Hera enters (p. 8), but they do not kiss the feet of their king or queen. The Hymn to Apollo opens with a description of how the gods react when Apollo arrives at the house of Zeus. They tremble and all dash from their seats as Apollo enters, stretching his bow, and only the god's mother, Leto, remains beside Zeus. She takes his bow away to hang up, and Zeus presents his son with a cup of nectar. Then the other gods resume their places, and Leto rejoices because she bore a powerful archer (verses 2–13). Apollo is a new god of whom the island of Delos can say before his birth that it is fearful to be the birth-place of Apollo, because it is reputed that Apollo will be very presumptuous and will rule mightily over gods and men (verses 66–9). The apprehension felt both by the other gods and by the island is hardly what we expect of a god often said to be the most Greek of all the Olympians, and a rumour which suggests that he was destined to usurp the prerogative of Zeus is more than a trifle surprising. It has been argued, therefore, that such ideas must be referred to an oriental source.[29] Marduk in Enuma Elish is a possible prototype, especially as the Hymn to Apollo tells the story of Apollo's birth and the origin of his sanctuary and festival on Delos. The Pythian part of the Hymn, whatever its date, depicts Apollo in the role of dragon-slayer. Finally, we should remember that the bow is Apollo's great weapon, while Enuma Elish makes the bow the weapon with which Marduk slays Tiamat (iv, 35 ff. and vi, 82–91). Whether or not the Hymn to Apollo is really two separate compositions, the fact that the Delian hymn must be close in date to Hesiod remains unchanged.[30] If its picture of Apollo owes anything to Marduk in Babylonian tradition, it is possible that the Theogony is not the only Greek poem composed towards the end of the eighth century B.C. which we may compare with Enuma Elish.

I have one last argument to advance. Enuma Elish rushes us into the story of the generations of the gods with nothing in the way of preliminary comment and no information about the author of the poem, who is, however, referred to as 'a leading figure' in the epilogue. But even if we know so little about the person who composed Enuma Elish, there is another Babylonian poem which helps us to understand the autobiographical passage at the beginning of the Theogony, and this is a work, furthermore, of late date. This text is the Epic of Era, a poem which has attracted much attention since Gössmann brought out a new edition of it in 1956.[31] Although it has yet to find a place in any of the standard collections of texts in translation, Kramer outlines its plot in *Mythologies*.[32]

Before anything is said about the Epic of Era, we must see what Hesiod has to tell us in the *prooemium* of the Theogony about how he came to be a poet. He was pasturing sheep beneath Mount Helicon when the Muses taught him beautiful song (verses 22 ff.). The first words which they addressed to their protégé warned him that they knew how to speak lies so dressed up that they seemed true and, when it took their fancy, how to tell the truth itself. They had Hesiod equip himself with a poet's staff and inspired him with song, requiring him to hymn the immortal gods and always to begin and end his composition with a reference to themselves. Hesiod sees no reason why he should proceed any further in describing what happened, but carries on with his poem, being careful, nevertheless, to put the instructions of the Muses into practice. The ancients had no hesitation in accepting such a picture, and to have been inspired while tending sheep became established as a literary convention. Now, however, we can be both romantic and scientific at the same time, for modern scholarship has revealed the presence in Greece of elements derived from a shamanistic level of culture, and thus made it easy for us to appreciate why a person like Hesiod or the poet-statesman Solon could hope to sway their countrymen.[33] And so we have come to realize that, for Hesiod at least, the appearance of the Muses is no literary conceit, but a description of something that Hesiod believed had actually taken place. Others might claim that the Muses had paid them a visit and keep their tongue firmly in their cheek when they said it, but for Hesiod the goddesses have a very real existence and form an active force in the life of mankind, especially if a man is a prince or a poet. The Heliconian Muses were sufficiently real for Hesiod to have dedicated to them the tripod which he won at the funeral games of Amphidamas of Chalcis (pp. 118–20).

One detail in the opening lines of the Theogony causes me to pause. It is generally assumed that what Hesiod experienced was an hallucination occurring in broad daylight while the poet was taking care of his sheep. The term hallucination is better than waking vision, since Hesiod nowhere says that he saw the Muses. Yet one reads in verses 9 ff. that it is during the night (ἐννύχιαι) that the goddesses, wrapped in thick mist, issue forth singing from the top of Helicon, and one begins to wonder, therefore, whether Hesiod is describing a dream and not something he experienced during the day. More certain is the arresting picture created by the poet; no one will deny that he succeeds in building up a tense atmosphere of suspense. The first two lines of the Theogony link together Muses and Helicon, while the next pair adds local colour in the shape of a spring and altar of Zeus. Then we have the actual names of springs – the Permessos, Horse's Spring, and Olmeios. Dancing gives way to song, as the Muses are said to quit the peak of Helicon at night. There is no formal description of the Muses, but a picture gradually forms in our minds when we read of their soft feet and tender bodies, the latter an expression which suggests Hesiod's description of the girl who avoids the inclement weather of winter by remaining indoors beside her mother (cf. Works and Days, 519 and 522). The first catalogue of the Theogony follows and then we find ourselves with Hesiod and his sheep. But the pace continues to gather momentum as the Muses address their enigmatic message to the poet and award to Hesiod a shoot of bay as a symbol of his new calling.

The possibility that Hesiod may be describing a dream-experience is important now that we are coming to consider the Near Eastern evidence. A first impression suggests that Babylonian literature is as anonymous as the Homeric poems. It is possible, however, to trace the use for centuries of particular names as family names where the family was of the guild type and its members originally followed the same occupation and were not necessarily related physically. Scribal families are known, and it would appear that these were the bodies transmitting Babylonian literature from the Cassite period onwards, when many of the standard works achieved a definitive form.[34] Comparable are the Greek Homeridai, for we know that these singers after a time were not restricted to the descendants of Homer, and that they existed at least as late as the fourth century B.C. Lately Lambert has published a new edition of a catalogue listing works and their authors from the library of Ashurbanipal.[35] The catalogue presents the results of critical research and not the arguments which led to those results. It certainly dates after 1000 B.C., and Lambert is of the opinion that it is probably not much older than Ashurbanipal himself. The first author whom it lists is the god Ea, while others, such as Adapa, Enmerkar, Enmedugga, and Lu-Nanna, though mortals, are men of legendary fame. We also have real men, either without mention of their family origin (presumably the older group) or described as 'son' of an ancestral figure. The catalogue represents a considerable achievement, one in fact, Lambert claims, comparable to modern discussion of the Homeric question, for the great majority of texts circulated without their author being named. The catalogue quotes the first line of the Era Epic and then mentions the name of its author. The gaps in the text, which include the name of the author, can be restored from the poem itself. But this does more than simply tell us the name of its author, since it also adds a precious little about the process of composition.

I do not wish to narrate at length the story told in the Epic of Era, but the date of the poem must be discussed and that means knowing something of its plot. The poem tells how the god of pestilence Era persuaded Marduk to evacuate Babylon and was thus able to lay waste the earth, including the great cities of Babylonia. He met strong opposition from his vizier Ishum and in the end was appeased by Ishum, ceasing from his work of destruction. The text concludes with a note of optimism when Era predicts prosperity and world conquest for the Akkadians. We seem here to have a reference to historical events, most probably the invasion of Mesopotamia by Aramean tribes known as the Sutu; these attacks we can date shortly after 1100 B.C. It took the country two hundred years to recover from the raids, and it was not until the ninth century that an avenger was found in the person of Nabu-apal-iddina, king of Babylon (*c.* 860 B.C.). After the final consolidation of Assyrian power in the middle of the eighth century B.C., it was no longer possible to hold out any hope that Babylonia might achieve imperial glory. This, therefore, imposes a lower limit on the date of composition of the Era Epic, and within the stretch of time between approximately 1050 and 750 B.C. the reign of Nabu-apal-iddina is the most likely period to have seen the poem composed.[36]

5

The fifth tablet of the epic, which opens with Era appeased, will be our concern. First Era speaks, pointing out how much the gods owe Ishum for having checked his wrath; next Ishum replies with a compliment which makes Era's face shine 'like a cloudless day'. Era calls Ishum 'to address an utterance to him, to instruct him concerning the scattered people of Akkad' (23–4).[37] This gives Era the opportunity to express a wish that this people become a great power once more. Quite suddenly at this point, two-thirds of the way through the fifth tablet, we read:

> Kabti-ili-Marduk, son of Dabibi, was the compiler of its tablets.
> It was revealed to him during the night, and when he spoke it in the morning, he did not leave out a single line,
> nor did he add one to it (42–4).

I suggest that in this passage we are faced with a poet's declaration of faith which, although much shorter, is of the same order as Hesiod's description of how he came to be visited by the Muses and inspired to sing. Both poets announce their names, both are inspired to sing of the gods, both perhaps receive their inspiration from a dream, and both seem anxious to affirm the reliability of their work. Kabti-ili-Marduk says that he neither omitted nor added a single line (cf. Odyssey iv, 349–50 and xvii, 140–1), and the Muses tell Hesiod that, when they want to, they can speak the truth. Did Kabti-ili-Marduk and his audience believe that inspiration could come in this way, or should we seek a more prosaic explanation? Unfortunately, the inspirational dream is a very rare motif in the literature of the Near East. In his fascinating study of the dream throughout the region, Oppenheim can quote only four examples, and two of these are our passages from Hesiod and the Epic of Era.[38] His third example, the Instruction of Amen-em-het, is to be discounted.[39] That leaves just a hymn to Sherua where it is stated that the goddess showed its author a vision during the night and he wrote these lines, placing his trust upon them. This is too slight to be of much assistance, although it does show that the claim made by Kabti-ili-Marduk was not unique in Babylonian literature.

We still have the last third of the fifth tablet of the Epic of Era to discuss. It is inevitable that this should be compared with the epilogue of Enuma Elish, the only equivalent as yet to be identified. In the creation poem all are invited to pay attention to the names of Marduk and so prosper. Marduk, it is said, is all-powerful, for 'reliable is his word, unalterable his command; the utterance of his mouth no god whatever can change' (vii, 151–2). It is Era again who speaks the closing lines of the other poem (49–61). Any god, king, and noble who praises the song or the god is wished the appropriate blessing; then this benediction is extended to embrace singer, scribe, and any house where a copy of the text is available, a fact which accounts for the popularity of the poem. Although plague rages, such a house will be untouched. The last three lines ask that the song may endure for ever and that everybody may hear it and praise the might of Era. Especially interesting is the list god, king, noble, singer, and scribe. About the last two the poem says:

> The singer who chants it shall not die in destruction,
> but his words shall be acceptable to king and noble.
> The scribe who commits it to memory, though he be held in contempt
> among the enemy, he shall be honoured in his own land (53–5).

Such, then, are the benefits granted by the god Era. In the *prooemium* of the Theogony Hesiod has something to tell us about the gifts which the Muses can bestow on two classes of men, kings and singers (verses 81 ff.). Both receive the gift of eloquence which enables a king to win admiration from his people as he judges disputes, and the singer to turn men's minds from thoughts of grief and anguish.

A copy of the first tablet and two small fragments of tablet two of the Epic of Era were found at Sultantepe. It would be a strange library which contained only part of a poem, and it must be assumed that the rest was there but has not been recovered. The same is true of the text of Enuma Elish from the same site, although in that case only tablet three is completely missing. Individualism was a new feature of Greek poetry composed towards the end of the eighth century B.C., and its first exponents were Hesiod and the author of the Delian part of the Apollo Hymn (cf. verses 166 ff.). Outside influence is one possible explanation of this development, and I have attempted to show that both the Theogony and the Hymn to Apollo were influenced by the tradition embodied in Enuma Elish. The Epic of Era contains a passage which is reminiscent of a very personal piece of Hesiod's autobiography. As neither Enuma Elish nor the Epic of Era appears to have been in existence while the Mycenaean civilization flourished, they could not have influenced the Greeks much before 800 B.C. If these clues are put together, what conclusion emerges? Unless every one of them is false, I think we must admit that in the eighth century B.C. the Near East influenced more than vase decoration, metalwork, and ivories among the Greeks, particularly when, in Hesiod's case, it is possible to trace a line of transmission from North Syria to the island of Euboea, a place which the poet claims to have visited. But this I shall have occasion to return to later, for I am now going beyond the subject of a chapter designed to consider the elements common to the Theogony and Enuma Elish and to evaluate other links between Greek and Babylonian literatures.

Chapter III

PANDORA AND THE
CREATION OF MANKIND

ENUMA Elish offers us a complete story of the creation. By complete I mean that it both tells the story of the generations of the gods and the rise to supreme power of their young king, and also accounts for the appearance of mankind. The creation of mankind is described at the beginning of the sixth tablet when it occurs as the final act in the story of creation. The tablet opens with Marduk revealing to Ea his intention of fashioning mankind in order that man may serve the gods.[1] It was the wise Ea who proposed the means to be employed, the execution of whatever god should be judged responsible for the outbreak of war by a jury comprising the gods gathered in assembly. Marduk thereupon summoned the gods together and invited them to deliver a verdict. They pronounced Kingu guilty, and this god was bound and held before Ea. His arteries were severed, and from the blood of Kingu mankind was created. According to Enuma Elish, therefore, man was created from divine blood and created expressly as the servant of the gods. In the catalogue of his names Marduk is said to have created mankind (vii, 29 and 32), but here, where we read the actual story of man's creation, Ea has usurped what we should expect to be more properly the function of Marduk, for, although Ea may act at his son's direction, the personal contribution of Marduk appears to be of a limited significance (see especially vi, 35–40). Such prominence on the part of Ea suggests that the author of Enuma Elish has drawn upon traditional material. To isolate this material, we must look for a version of the story with Ea and not Marduk cast in the main role.

What was the standard account of man's creation among the Babylonians? A variety of texts from Mesopotamia contains passing references to the event. Thus the Sumerian Myth of the Pickaxe implies that, according to one tradition, man shot up like a plant from the ground through a hole made by the god Enlil.[2] On a bilingual tablet the same idea, that man grew out of the earth, occurs in line twenty of the reverse. The obverse of the tablet, however, seems to tell a different story: how, after the basic work of creating the world had been finished, the gods discussed among themselves what they were to do next, and it was suggested to Enlil that craftsmen gods should be slain and mankind be created from their blood to serve the gods.[3] Perhaps, as Lambert conjectures, the blood was used to water the ground whence man came forth. Line nineteen in the Myth of the Pickaxe, where we read that Enlil 'put human slaves in the mould', suggests another material and another technique, the creation of mankind from clay in the same way as a craftsman shapes a figurine. In the Theodicy it is said:

> Narru, king of the gods, who created mankind,
> and majestic Zulummar, who dug out their clay,
> and mistress Mami, the queen who fashioned them,
> gave perverse speech to the human race (276–9).[4]

The three deities, Narru, Zulummar, and Mami, are better known as Enlil, Ea, and Aruru (the Mother-goddess). Earlier in the same work Aruru is called creator (line 258), while the Poem of the Righteous Sufferer describes mortals as 'creatures whose clay Aruru took in her fingers' (iv, 40).[5] In the Epic of Gilgamesh the same goddess created Enkidu, pinching off clay and casting it on the steppe; in his law code Hammurabi describes himself in the prologue as 'the one whom the sage, Mama, brought to perfection', and in the epilogue makes Nintu 'the mother who bore me'.[6] Both Mama and Nintu are the Mother-goddess. An incantation myth credits the combined efforts of Marduk and Aruru with the creation of mankind (lines 20–1).[7]

These references can be supplemented by the full story as we know it from the Sumerian Myth of Enki and Ninmah and from the Babylonian Epic of Atrahasis. The former opens with the gods in distress because of the difficulty which they were experiencing in obtaining food now that their numbers were increased.[8] They complained through his mother Nammu (p. 38) to Enki, the Sumerian form of Ea, who first created seven birth-goddesses and then revealed to Nammu the following plan: he proposed to mix clay and his own blood, while the birth-goddesses were to nip off pieces of the clay and with these Nammu was to shape bodies; Ninmah, the Mother-goddess, was also required to help in the process. When this was complete, Nammu had to assign to the creatures thus produced their function in the universe, and Ninmah to impose upon them the burden of feeding the gods. We know today that the Atrahasis Epic related the story of all mankind and not merely that of the hero of the flood; it began with an account of man's creation of which the Old Babylonian version is preserved, and went on to recount all of man's subsequent history as far as the survival of

Atrahasis.[9] Man was once again created to relieve the pressure on the gods. Mami, when invited to create mankind, claimed that it was impossible for her to do this unaided and called on Enki for assistance. Rather than use his own, Enki had a god put to death in order to supply flesh and blood, and these substances were mixed together either by themselves or with clay. The resultant compound was then treated by Enki, who trod it like a potter, by Mami, who nipped off fourteen pieces of the clay, and by the birth-goddesses, who, taking one piece of clay each, made seven pairs of humans. After a nine-month period of gestation, the new creatures stepped forth from a 'womb'. This tradition provided the Babylonians with their standard account of man's creation, although variations are found, as in the passage from the Theodicy quoted above. Both clay as an ingredient and the Mother-goddess and the birth-goddesses are missing from the story as we meet it in Enuma Elish, but Ea keeps his traditional position. Lambert suggests that the author of Enuma Elish may have been too sophisticated for the idea that man was created as a pot or a figurine is created to have any appeal.

Before we reach the end of the Theogony we learn of gods, like Zeus and Dionysos, who mate with mortal women, and, in the closing lines of the poem, of unions between goddesses and men. If Zeus had not been quick to perceive Typhoeus, the dragon would have made himself lord of men and gods (verses 836–8). But a considerable time before we come to the story of Typhoeus, the existence of mankind is taken for granted in Hesiod's story of Prometheus and Pandora. This begins halfway through the Theogony with trouble between men and gods at Mekone (verses 535 ff.): Prometheus tricked Zeus in the matter of the sacrificial meat, and the god took his revenge by denying mankind the benefit of fire; Prometheus persisted in his opposition to Zeus and stole fire, but Zeus had the last word when he ordered the preparation of the first woman. It has been suggested that the Hittite myths may, like the Theogony, assume the presence of men on earth, although the story of their creation was not included in the Kumarbi cycle. In an isolated fragment which may or may not belong to the Song of Ullikummi, the god Ea points out that the annihilation of mankind would force the gods to do all the work of providing for themselves.[10] In the KAL text Ea complains to Kumarbi and later tells his vizier to report to Nara, the brother of Ea, that KAL is rebellious himself and has also 'made the countries rebellious, and no one any longer gives bread or drink offerings to the gods'.[11] The evidence of the KAL text, however, is as uncertain as that of the isolated fragment, and will remain so until the relation of the KAL text to the Kumarbi cycle is established.

Hesiod's story of Prometheus and Pandora has fascinated scholars to no lesser extent than it did the poet himself. Before, therefore, we examine at length the section describing the preparation of the first woman, I must discuss the whole of this episode from the Theogony.[12] It begins with a list of the offspring of Iapetos and Klymene (verses 507 ff.). Immediately before we have seen Kronos supplanted by Zeus, and now we pass on to the children of Iapetos, another son of Ouranos and Gaia (verse 134); they were four in number – Atlas, Menoitios, Prometheus, and Epimetheus. At the very beginning we anticipate the end of the Pandora story as we know it from the Works and Days by means of a brief reference to Epimetheus' reception of the first woman (verses 512–4). In reverse order we read of the various disasters which overtook the stupid Epimetheus, the outrageous Menoitios, and Atlas who 'of hard necessity' carries the heavens on his head and hands.[13] Although Atlas is called stout-hearted in verse 509, this is hardly to be regarded as a compliment, since the same adjective is applied elsewhere in the Theogony to Echidna and her children (verses 297 and 308), while in the Works and Days it qualifies the θυμός of the bronze age men (verse 147). The reverse order, however, is broken in the case of Prometheus, the only son of Iapetos whose story is developed. I see no contradiction between the verses here which describe Prometheus being released by Heracles and the epilogue to the episode as a whole (verses 614–6). The lines which close the episode may say that for all his cunning a mighty chain binds the Titan, but they represent the poet's judgment on the entire story of deceit and retribution, being comprised of the proverb of verse 613 (cf. Works and Days, 105) and the application of its warning to the case of Prometheus. This is a general comment, and there is no conflict between Hesiod's choice of a vivid present and his earlier description of Prometheus set free. Before Hesiod lists the sons of Iapetos, we have the release of his father's brothers by Zeus mentioned (verses 501–6), and later the Centomani help Zeus against the Titans. Prometheus is another of the older gods who was first imprisoned and then released, and Heracles does for Prometheus what his father does for the Cyclopes, but without acting, like Prometheus, in defiance of Zeus. Indeed Hesiod finds a reason why Zeus should permit the release of Prometheus (verses 529–34), just as, slightly later, he offers an explanation as to how Zeus came to make the wrong choice in the matter of the sacrifice (verses 550–2), a passage where we see a second aetiology (verses 556–7) to match that of verses 498–500.

Prometheus' first crime against Zeus was to trick the king of the gods into selecting the inferior part of the sacrificial meat. The trick reveals the subtlety of Prometheus: he presented Zeus with the better portion, whereas men were offered the bare bones carefully decked out with fat so as to appear the more attractive share; Zeus fell into the trap, complained, and insisted on making his own choice, only to find that what he eventually received was in fact the bones.[14] The first words of Zeus to Prometheus were heavily charged with an unconscious irony (verses 543–4); they were uttered reproachfully, while Prometheus replied with guile (verses 548–9). But anger seized the god when Zeus saw himself made to look a fool and he spoke a second time (verses 559–60), and anger is the dominant emotion displayed by Zeus (cf. verses 533, 554, 558, 561, and 567–8). Zeus is extremely annoyed and so he does not turn the other cheek, but hits back at Prometheus as hard as he can. I fail to see how it can be seriously argued that Zeus in this story is really a god of great wisdom, intent on pursuing a policy of educating mankind through hardships.[15] The god's behaviour is governed by the principle of self-assertion which forces an injured person to exact revenge or be discredited. This is a code of morality which not only allows the injured party to avenge himself, but even demands retribution if a loss of face is threatened. If Zeus here is a cruel god, it is the Titan and mankind who are to blame; they insulted the majesty of Zeus, and by such a standard Zeus would be less than a great god if he failed to retaliate. Mankind is as guilty as Prometheus, for we remember that, according to the Works and Days, one evil man can blight a whole city (verses 240–1).

But the standards of shame culture pose a problem for a poet such as Hesiod, convinced of the justice of Zeus. A good illustration is provided by Hesiod's stories of the dynastic changes in heaven. When Gaia urged her children to take action against their father Ouranos, she stressed the fact that Ouranos had been the first to commit foul deeds, and, in his reply to Gaia, Kronos voiced the same sentiment (verses 166 and 172). The situation repeats itself in almost the same words in the Odyssey at the palace of Odysseus, where the suitors, as they prepare their fatal last supper, receive no sympathy from the poet, for they again had been the first to stoop to violence (xx, 394), and so Odysseus has ample justification for the terrible revenge he is to take upon them. But Kronos' treatment of his father does not close the cycle of crime and punishment, for Ouranos is said to have called his sons Titans because they had strained (τιταίνοντας) to do a monstrous deed for which revenge would follow (verses 207–10), and among those born from the severed genitals of Ouranos were the Erinyes. Rhea was helped by Gaia and Ouranos to give birth to Zeus in safety so she could revenge not only the children swallowed by Kronos, but the *erinyes* of her father as well (verses 472–3). Although the crimes committed by Ouranos and by Kronos against their own children are very much alike, Zeus is not punished for deposing his father, and, when his rule is in danger, we find Gaia and Ouranos the allies of the reigning power (verses 891–3). Yet Hesiod would have us believe that children should respect their parents, and he considers the fact that children are like their parents a sign of the just city. A change to a new code of ethics can be awkward, and this may be another reason why Hesiod concentrates on the story of the birth of Zeus, but says little about the actual overthrow of Kronos.

Three two-line passages of direct speech occur in Hesiod's story of Prometheus, and they form an obvious pattern which is emphasized by the sequence of speakers – Zeus, Prometheus, and then Zeus once more – and by a use of repetition (cf. verses 545, 550, 559, and 561; 547 and 560; and 540, 555, and 557). Prometheus went on to commit another crime by stealing fire, which Zeus now denied to mankind. The king of the gods next had Hephaistos and Athene prepare the first woman, who is not given a name in the Theogony. This beautiful creature and Prometheus' collection of bones dressed up in fat spell out the same moral lesson, the folly of basing a judgment on external appearance by itself, for beauty is always likely to be no more than skin deep, and something may look attractive but really be deadly. Epimetheus and Zeus fall victim to an identical trick, and Zeus, therefore, pays his enemies back in their own coin by an act of deceit which is comparable but much more crushing. Again we can see a play on words in the metric position of προέθηκε in verse 537, κατέθηκε in 539 and 541, περίθηκε in 577, and ἐνέθηκε in 583; and εὐθετίσας in 541 and ἀσκήσας in 580. Hesiod, however, carries his story of the first woman no further, but turns aside to deliver a savage attack on the female sex (verses 590 ff.) before he rounds off this part of his poem with the general epilogue of verses 613–6. A series of short speeches, therefore, characteristically occupies a central position in the narrative, while an attempt by Prometheus to deceive Zeus stands on either side of the speeches: the preparation of the first woman repeats the Titan's initial trick against Zeus.

The corresponding story, as related in the Works and Days, is different in a number of respects.[16] There the woman is given her name of Pandora, and more deities than Hephaistos and Athene join in producing her. It is possible that the words of Zeus in verses 54–8 imply that Pandora in the Works and Days, as in the Theogony, is to be regarded as an evil in herself apart from the fatal but very feminine curiosity which caused her to open the jar and release disaster upon mankind. At first sight the only hint of this stage in the story that we meet in the Theogony comes in Hesiod's catalogue of the sons of Iapetos and the misfortunes which befell them. But perhaps we may detect an echo of Pandora's jar in the later description of Tartarus. Elsewhere I have attempted to show that Pandora's jar is a magic pot made of metal and most probably of bronze.[17] It is a container from which nothing can escape because magic has made the jar unbreakable (cf. verse 96). But the lid may be removed and the spell thus rendered ineffective, and Pandora is silly enough to do this. We are wrong to compare the pithoi of Zeus which, according to the Iliad, stand on the threshold of Zeus (xxiv, 527 ff.), for what we want is a jar used as a place of imprisonment and not simply because it affords storage facilities. The proper Homeric parallel is provided by the bronze jar in which Otos and Ephialtes shut away the god Ares for thirteen months (Iliad v, 385–91). But the jar in which Ares was locked up has long been quoted to elucidate a problem in Hesiod's description of Tartarus, namely verses 726–7, where it is said that a bronze fence surrounds Tartarus and night is poured in three rows about its neck. Stokes, the latest person to discuss what Hesiod means by the neck of Tartarus, shows that the word δειρή has to be taken in the sense of neck, but ignores a suggestion made by Aly and repeated by Mazon.[18] Aly claimed that neck here was to be thought of as the neck of a pithos, while Mazon remarked that Tartarus was represented as a kind of pot. The connection between a jar and the underworld has been discussed by Wagenvoort in a study of the Latin word *orcus*.[19] This scholar believes that *Orcus* as the name of a god is a secondary development, and that basically it is the name of the underworld which was depicted as a type of pitcher with a narrow neck (cf. *orca*). The reference to the neck of Tartarus made by Hesiod in the passage under discussion suggests that the Greeks as well as the Romans shared such a belief. If the underworld was conceived of as a pot, the Theogony may not be wholly uninfluenced by the later stages of the Pandora story as we know them from the other poem by Hesiod.

But there is another difference between the versions of the Pandora story in the Theogony and the Works and Days: they serve a very different purpose. In the Works and Days the history of Prometheus and Pandora explains why we should have to toil to support life in a world controlled by a supposedly benevolent Zeus. Perses will ask why the god allows our existence to be dominated by the necessity of work, and Hesiod has a convenient answer ready in this story or in that of the five ages of mankind. The first answer teaches more than the alternative explanation, since it also offers a classic example of what can happen to a fool who decides to ignore the advice of a wiser brother. Prometheus told Epimetheus not to accept any present sent him by Zeus but to return it. Yet Epimetheus received Pandora and realized his mistake only when it was too late (verses 85–9). If you personally are not wise, it is possible to take advice from somebody who is; if you cannot see the true situation for yourself and will not listen to another's words of wisdom, then you are utterly useless (verses 293–7). But we ought not to strain our analogy, for, while his stupidity makes Perses the counterpart of Epimetheus, he also resembles the clever brother Prometheus in one respect: in trying to corrupt Dike, the daughter of Zeus, Perses is following the bad example set mankind by Prometheus, and no one, including a Titan, is able to deceive Zeus. In the Works and Days Hesiod has to cover both the reason why man has to sweat and toil and the appalling consequences of rejecting sound advice, and it is in order to meet the needs of the immediate context that he tells the story of Pandora's jar and the escape of its contents.

The Theogony, on the other hand, describes the creation, and its story of Prometheus, therefore, culminates in the creation of the first woman. The evil is now Pandora in her capacity as a woman, and, as Hesiod does not wish to justify work, there is no point in sketching the history of her misdemeanours once she had been received on earth. A necessary supplement to the birth of the gods is the appearance on earth of their human worshippers. The version of the story told in the Theogony accounts for the origin of at least one of the two sexes, while the present existence of the other along with the gods is assumed; this occurs, furthermore, at the central point in the poem. I could leave the matter here, but, I must admit, with no great satisfaction. While I believe all I have just said to be valid, I have always wondered whether Hesiod had some special reason for choosing this particular story. The myth of the ages in the Works and Days, whatever verse 108 may or may not mean, proves that another tradition about the origin of the human race was known to Hesiod: in that myth the ages of gold, silver, bronze, and the heroes are the work of the Olympians collectively or Zeus alone (verses 109–10, 127–8, 143–4, and 157–9); in addition the men of the third age are said to have been fashioned from ash-trees (verse 145). According to Apollodorus, Prometheus moulded men from water and earth (1, 7, 1), but such a tradition begins only in the fourth century B.C. and represents a development of Hesiod's own story of Prometheus. The gap in Hesiod's narrative was felt, and it was filled by making Prometheus, already the great benefactor of mankind, its creator also. Prometheus was the father of Deukalion, and a fragment from the Catalogue (Rzach 115) refers to the repopulation of the earth after the flood. This, however, does not allow us to assume that Hesiod considered Prometheus the creator of mankind. We are left, therefore, still asking ourselves why Hesiod chose the Pandora story as the means of introducing the human race into his poem. Was the Pandora story perhaps already associated with the myth of creation, and, if so, how? The Near East may help us to find an answer.

There is a second problem on which the comparative material throws some light, and I can best illustrate this and also link up with the Near Eastern evidence, if I examine what Hesiod has to say about the preparation of Pandora. In the Theogony the preparation of Pandora follows Prometheus' theft of fire (verses 570 ff.). At the instruction of Zeus Hephaistos moulded from earth the likeness of a maiden, and the goddess Athene equipped the woman thus produced with a splendid array of clothes. Most spectacular was the head-gear, which consisted of a veil, garlands of flowers, and a golden diadem made by Hephaistos himself and decorated with a design featuring many of the creatures reared on land and in the sea. These were so skilfully rendered that they seemed alive. Pandora is called a beautiful evil (verse 585), an expression also applicable to the poorer part of the sacrifice, and it is her head-gear, the outward manifestation of her beauty, and not the actual creation of the girl which claims Hesiod's attention. The account given in the Works and Days is more elaborate. There we start with the orders of Zeus (verses 60 ff.), when Hephaistos is required to fashion Pandora, using a mixture of earth and water, and to produce a human equivalent of the immortal goddesses.[20] Zeus tells Athene to teach Pandora womanly skills such as weaving, while Aphrodite must endow her with charm and the power of seduction. Hermes has also to participate, and his contribution is to be a mind devoid of scruples and a nature compounded of stealth. When the orders are put into effect, the picture becomes even more complicated: Hephaistos makes Pandora from earth and Athene dresses her; Aphrodite vanishes, but the Graces, Peitho, and the Horai provide gold necklaces and a crown of spring flowers, ornaments which might be thought lavish enough but nothing like the glorious head-gear described in the Theogony; Hermes adds lies, crafty words, treacherous heart, and voice, the last being an obvious complement to his other gifts. Thus, in comparison with the Theogony, we have an expansion in both the number of gods concerned and the range of gifts they bestow. But Hesiod has a clear motive for doing this: in the Works and Days we learn that the girl's name is Pandora, and that she received her name from Hermes because all the Olympians gave her a present (verses 80–2). Hesiod could hardly have said that all the gods gave her a present, if it was only Hephaistos and Athene who carried out their father's commands, and more gods have to be included in order to make sense of Hesiod's explanation of the name. This, then, is no problem, but the crown described so carefully in the Theogony is more difficult. Hesiod must give his first woman all the trappings of external beauty, but he concentrates exclusively on her head-gear, especially the crown prepared by Hephaistos. Since the Works and Days ignores this altogether, one is left speculating whether the crown has any special significance for the Theogony. Does the Near East help us to understand the significance of the crown in addition to answering the main question of how the story of Pandora became part of a creation text?

Hesiod has Hephaistos fashion Pandora from earth or by using a mixture of earth and water (cf. also Iliad vii, 99). It has long been recognized that here we have something very like the process which we encountered at the beginning of this chapter when we surveyed Babylonian accounts of the creation of man: Hephaistos is conceived of as a craftsman building up a figure from clay. Thus, many years ago, Paley in a note on verse 61 of the Works and Days remarked that 'there is evidently an allusion to the primitive fictile statuettes, or to sculptors' clay models'. But there is one thing missing from the Babylonian texts, for it will be remembered that they are not consistent in naming the god who fashioned mankind, although the standard tradition makes it Ea and the Mother-goddess. There is, however, no mention of a craftsman god of the type represented by the Greek Hephaistos, and in our search for a parallel from the Near East we need to locate a craftsman god who creates mankind. In chapter two I referred to one god falling into such a category, the Ugaritic Kathir-and-Khasis, who provided Baal with the weapons necessary to crush Yam (p. 31), but the texts from Ugarit contain no account of the origin of mankind. Philo of Byblos knew Kathir-and-Khasis, since he refers to two brothers who discovered iron and how to work it; one of the brothers, moreover, according to Philo, corresponded to Hephaistos. But Philo's first mortal men, Aion and Protogonos, the offspring of the wind Kolpia and his wife Baau, get us nowhere.[21] We have not, however, exhausted all the possibilities, for there was in the Near East a celebrated craftsman god who was also considered the creator of mankind: the Egyptian ram-headed god Khnum was thought to fashion living creatures on the potter's wheel in much the same way as Aruru made Enkidu and Hephaistos prepared Pandora. This is a clue I want to pursue, but now that we find ourselves having to discuss an Egyptian god, we seem to be faced with yet a further collection of texts. We have already examined the Hittite and Babylonian material, and now I propose to go on to Egypt and introduce still more evidence of possible influence on Hesiod. But it has been inevitable from the first page of chapter one that something should be said about Egyptian ideas, for Nilsson, when he originally dismissed the Kumarbi myth as the prototype of the Theogony, suggested that Egyptian tradition was the place for us to look (p. 1). But let us leave on one side for the present Egyptian accounts of the creation of the universe, so that we may devote all our attention to the clue offered by a craftsman god commonly called the fashioner of man and one whose name may reflect such a function.[22]

So far we have Egypt and Khnum, but it would be an advantage if we could narrow down the limits of our investigation. Pandora qualifies as something very special, and this suggests that we ought to restrict our search among the Egyptian material to evidence which also relates to the creation of something of a special nature. What did the Egyptians consider more special than their kings? The answer surely is nothing, and so the particular question we must ask is the following one: how did the Egyptians regard the coming into existence of a new manifestation of Horus? Furthermore, was the god Khnum thought to play any part in the birth of a pharaoh? Curiously enough some of our best evidence concerns a woman, but this appears to be largely a matter of accident. At the beginning of the fifteenth century B.C. Egypt was ruled for some twenty years by that remarkable woman Hatshepsut. Many would claim as the outstanding memorial of her reign the staggering mortuary temple constructed on the left bank of the Nile at

Deir el-Bahari. The temple has often been described and we shall be interested in only a small part of it, the northern half of the middle colonnade, where a series of reliefs, accompanied by inscriptions, records the story of the birth and coronation of Queen Hatshepsut.[23] Although they were deliberately defaced by two later pharaohs, the gaps may be filled by combining the evidence provided by comparable scenes and inscriptions which portray the same events in the life of Amenhotep III; these are to be found in his temple of Amon at Luxor. I cannot expect to do justice to the reliefs from Hatshepsut's temple, but I must attempt a brief description of them, if I am to present their evidence fairly. Naturally, I shall say most about those scenes which are relevant to the Pandora story. The first relief shows a council of the gods over which Amon is presiding, while the second and third scenes depict an interview between Amon and Thoth and the two gods hand in hand. Their destination is made obvious by the next relief, a picture of Amon and Queen Ahmose, the wife of Thutmose I, sitting opposite one another. An inscription tells us what is taking place: it seems that Amon assumed the outward appearance of Thutmose I, the reigning pharaoh, and visited the queen in the palace; the fragrance of the god aroused Ahmose from her sleep, and they were joined together. 'He caused that she should see him in his form of a god. When he came before her, she rejoiced at the sight of his beauty, his love passed into her limbs, which the fragrance of the god flooded; all his odours were from Punt.' Another inscription records an exchange between the queen and her divine lover, and in this Amon announces the name and power of the child to be born as a result of their union.[24]

The first part of the story told in the reliefs reveals the existence in Egypt of a tradition according to which the chief god disguises himself as a mortal husband and enjoys the favours of that person's wife. A popular tale known from the Papyrus Westcar confirms the existence of such a tradition. The Papyrus Westcar tells a story of Herodotean charm: it relates how the pharaoh Cheops once amused himself by listening to his sons telling stories of the great magicians of the past.[25] While doing this, he learnt of a magician who was still alive. The magician was accordingly summoned to appear before the king, where he proved his worth by performing a number of miracles. Then he uttered a prophecy that the pharaoh's family would be overthrown and a new dynasty establish itself on the throne of Egypt. Three children were to be born to a woman named Rededet, the wife of a priest of Re. Their father was the god Re himself, who had told Rededet that their offspring would exercise supreme power in the land. The story continues by relating how, when the woman was in labour, Re despatched five deities to deliver the children and to ensure they were safely born. Although the tale is set in the reign of Cheops and refers to the transition from fourth to fifth dynasty, our text of it is much later, being generally thought to date from the beginning of the eighteenth dynasty or about half a century before the accession of Hatshepsut. The Greeks were fully aware of the amorous propensities of Zeus and his fellow gods. The birth of Heracles closely parallels that of Hatshepsut inasmuch as Zeus had his way with Alkmene, having assumed the likeness of her husband Amphitryon.[26] Other women were seduced by Zeus, who appeared in the form of an animal, bird, or, in the case of Danae, a shower of golden rain. The last disguise ceases to be a puzzle once we remember the significance of gold in Egyptian thought: it is the royal metal (compare the men of the golden age in the Works and Days), and gold forms the flesh of the gods.[27] Fragrance was a characteristic of the Greek gods: thus in the Hymn to Demeter, when the goddess revealed herself to Metaneira and changed from an old woman back into her true shape, 'from her perfumed robes there spread a lovely fragrance' (verses 277–8).

The next group of scenes from Deir el-Bahari is especially important. The first scene, the fifth relief in the series, features Amon and the ram-headed Khnum. From an inscription at Luxor we learn the purport of Amon's orders to Khnum: 'Go, to make her, together with her ka, from these limbs which are in me; go, to fashion her better than all gods; shape for me, this my daughter, whom I have begotten. I have given to her all life and satisfaction, all stability, all joy of heart from me, all offerings, and all bread, like Re, forever'.[28] Khnum expresses every willingness to comply with his instructions. The following picture shows Khnum actually shaping Hatshepsut and her ka, both of whom are represented by a male child, on what is usually taken to be a potter's wheel.[29] On one side kneels the wife of Khnum, the frog-headed goddess Heqet, who holds out before the nostrils of the two children the symbol of life. In an inscription Khnum repeats the orders of Amon, although the correspondence is not an exact one. We may hurry over the next reliefs where we have an interview between Thoth and the queen, Khnum and Heqet leading Ahmose to her place of confinement, and the birth itself. In the birth scene Ahmose, holding the child and attended by divinities, sits on a throne placed on an immense couch. Then we see the goddess Hathor presenting Hatshepsut to her father Amon, Amon, who is now holding the child, and Hathor together, each on a throne, and a scene where child and ka are suckled by the gods. This part of the story ends with three more reliefs, the first of which depicts two gods presenting child and ka to the gods, here represented by three anonymous figures, while in the second Thoth presents the pair to Amon.

→ The wall decorated with these pictures is about fifteen feet in height; it is divided into two registers of equal height; the reliefs so far described form the lower series. Those in the upper register continue the story of Hatshepsut after she has been brought into the world. We commence with a relief on which Amon and another god purify Hatshepsut by pouring water over her head. Then we see Amon sitting on a throne and holding his daughter on his knees; he is presenting the child to all the gods of Egypt, who accept her and acknowledge her supremacy. The next scene portrays a journey to the North made by Hatshepsut to receive the approval of the gods. By this time Hatshepsut had grown into a beautiful maiden, and, to quote the inscription, 'her form was like a god, she did everything as a god, her splendour was like a god; her majesty was a maiden, beautiful, blooming, Buto in her time'.[30] The two reliefs which follow have as their subject the crowning of Hatshepsut, first by Atum, the god of Heliopolis, and then by Amon. The next scene, which is almost entirely destroyed, showed Hatshepsut receiving her royal titles from the gods. This part of the coronation is completed by a picture of Hatshepsut, now dressed as Pharaoh and wearing the double crown of Upper and Lower Egypt, standing before Amon. The corresponding ceremonies on earth are depicted in a relief which shows Hatshepsut standing before the enthroned figure of her putative father, Thutmose I, in the presence of the royal court. A series of inscriptions accompanies the picture: in the first Thutmose addresses his daughter, calling on her to be crowned; the second records how the pharaoh summoned the court to do homage before Hatshepsut; the third preserves the words in which Thutmose announced to the courtiers that Hatshepsut was his successor; in the fourth we read how the court replied with rejoicing; finally the new queen's names are proclaimed. The reliefs conclude with a second act of purification and other ceremonies performed by the gods.

But what does all this mean where Hesiod's Pandora is concerned? It seems to me that here, in the pictures from Deir el-Bahari, is the closest parallel to the description of the preparation of Pandora in the Theogony. It is a parallel, moreover, which we can explain in terms of both transmission of influence and significance. In the Theogony Zeus has Pandora made ready by the craftsman god Hephaistos. At our Egyptian temple Amon requires Khnum to produce Hatshepsut, and the work is completed by the craftsman god, assisted by his wife Heqet, who extends to infant and ka the symbol of life. One recalls how Athene joins Hephaistos in carrying out the plan of Zeus, especially as, according to Hyginus (Fab. 142), *Vulcanus Iouis iussu ex luto mulieris effigiem fecit, cui Minerua animam dedit.* Khnum and Hephaistos appear to work using a similar technique, one employing the potter's wheel and the other taking clay as his raw material.[31] Hesiod makes much of Pandora's head-dress, and one would dearly love to date the golden diadem. But when the difficulty of deciding on the right date for jewellery such as the Aegina Treasure is considered, chances seem forlorn.[32] The best that can be said at present is that its type of decoration suggests an eighth-century gold band with an animal frieze motif.[33] If, however, a connection with Hatshepsut's reliefs is allowed, it is possible to see why this item in Pandora's ornamentation should have received special mention, for the second part of the Egyptian queen's story concentrates on her coronation in heaven and on earth, and her coronation is the decisive moment in her assumption of power.[34] When Pandora had been prepared, she was led out to where the other gods and men were assembled, and her gorgeous appearance caused them to be overwhelmed with wonder. Hatshepsut is also presented to both gods and men, and in both instances we are left in no doubt as to the remarkable beauty of the handiwork of the gods. A link between the royal ideology of the Egyptians and Pandora means that we are in a position to vindicate the etymology of the name Pandora as Hesiod explains it in the Works and Days. Hermes called the girl Pandora because all the gods had given her a gift (verses 80–2), while the Egyptians believed that the gods granted all gifts to the reigning pharaoh.[35]

I appreciate that my readers may by this time be experiencing a surprise not unlike that felt by gods and men when they first cast their eyes on the beautiful Pandora. The parallel which I have identified will, however, be much easier to accept, if answers can be found to two questions: first, what evidence is there to suggest that the Greeks knew and were influenced by the Egyptian concept of kingship? Then, secondly, can we trace any connection between the creation myth and the story of a king's birth and coronation? The first of the questions is the easier one to answer, and so I shall begin by asking how and when it was possible for the Greeks to have become acquainted with the idea that kings were created by the gods and to have adopted such an idea themselves.

Two lines of argument can be developed, one assuming an indirect and the other a direct influence on the Greeks. If the influence was indirect, it would have spread northwards from Egypt into the general area of Palestine and Syria, and from there made its way to Greece. This argument depends upon our proving that a comparable concept of kingship and one, furthermore, ultimately derived from Egypt existed in Palestine and Syria. The evidence which supports such a theory has been collected and discussed by Widengren, who refers to the Genesis story of how a son came to be born to Abraham and Sarah, pointing out that the name Sarah is generally thought to be the same as the Akkadian word for queen or princess, while, when Yahweh is said to visit Sarah, it is possible that the word 'visit' here has a sexual connotation.[36] His interpretation of the story means that we are faced with 'an Israelitic adaptation of an ancient Canaanite tradition of the visit of a deity to the queen'. The Canaanite background of the tradition is suggested by the texts from Ugarit, wherein Widengren identifies birth-oracles including the same stylistic features also to be found in the birth-oracle which God gave to Abraham, I should add at this point that the divine status of the kings of Ugarit has since been confirmed by the discovery of a text listing the names of fourteen kings of Ugarit where each name is preceded by the word for god.[37] Behind the Ugaritic texts and Hebrew myth Widengren sees the influence of Egypt and its attitude towards the pharaoh as we know it from the Deir el-Bahari reliefs, for in the words of Amon to Queen Ahmose, when the name of the divine child is announced and a prediction as to its future power made, we again have a characteristic birth-oracle. I have already compared the story of the birth of Heracles with that of Hatshepsut (p. 67); birth-oracles are also associated with the Greek hero. Thus Diodorus tells us that even before the birth of Heracles the excessive strength of the child was presaged by the fact that Zeus made the night of his conception three times the normal length (4, 9, 2). Reading on, we find that, when Alkmene's period of pregnancy was complete, Zeus made an announcement in the presence of all the gods that he proposed to make the child born on that day king over the descendants of Perseus (4, 9, 4). Long before Diodorus, moreover, we see the birth-oracle as part of the Heracles legend as it is recorded in the Iliad (xix, 101–5).

It is possible, therefore, that the Deir el-Bahari tradition, like so much else, was passed on to the Greeks via Syria. But I myself prefer the alternative of direct contact between Egypt and the Greeks in the period after about 1570 B.C. There is a considerable body of evidence to suggest that the Mycenaean kings were sacral kings in the full Egyptian sense, and one may draw on mythology, archaeology, and literature to substantiate the hypothesis. I have no intention of covering the whole field of evidence, but I shall select a few examples in an attempt to demonstrate that the Egyptian pattern of monarchy was reproduced by that of the Mycenaean world, and that the tradition embodied in the pictures from Deir el-Bahari was taken over by the Greeks directly in Late Helladic times. The Pandora story in Hesiod, in my opinion, owes something to pre-Dorian Greece and should be considered with our other evidence for Mycenaean survivals in Greek epic.

Mythological evidence of Egyptian influence on Mycenae and its civilization is offered by the story of Danaos and his flight from Egypt. Some believe that mythology can prove anything, and others nothing. But with Danaos, Shaft-Grave Circle A, and the expulsion of the Hyksos from Egypt we do seem to have some connection, although we cannot be certain what that connection is. Opinion is divided between regarding Danaos as a displaced Hyksos who carved a new kingdom out for himself in the Argolid, or as a mercenary who fought on the Egyptian side against the Hyksos and, having returned to Greece, introduced into his native land much of what he had seen overseas.[38] Egypt thus influenced both the material culture and the ideas of the Mycenaeans. Among those to support the mercenary theory is the Greek archaeologist Marinatos. One of the finds from the shaft graves at Mycenae which he has referred to Egyptian art is the famous cup that we have become accustomed to compare with Nestor's cup in the Iliad. Marinatos claims that the birds on its handles are Egyptian Horus falcons and that they serve to symbolize the divine king whose cup this was.[39] This would be an idea which the Greeks adopted from the royal ideology of Egypt. One of the descendants of Danaos was Perseus, whose birth I mentioned above when referring to Greek versions of the divine child type of myth (p. 67). Nilsson believes that the scenes on the Hagia Triada sarcophagus mean that the Mycenaean king was worshipped after his death as a god.[40] The beehive tombs of Mycenae in all their stark grandeur certainly appear to indicate sumptuous rites. If Palmer is right, Pylos has yielded among its Linear B tablets a tomb inventory whose furniture finds its nearest parallel in that recovered from the tomb of Tut-ankh-Amon, though the person buried at Pylos was not the *wanax*.[41]

While the sheer accumulation of data is impressive in itself, none of it is without its difficulties, and there is still no general agreement as to the status of the Mycenaean king. Was the *wanax* regarded as a god or just god's representative on earth? Guthrie prefers the second possibility, since he sees no evidence in the Linear B tablets to show that the king was thought a god while alive. He further argues that the shrines in the palaces were dedicated to a goddess, and, therefore, suggest a mortal king who needed divine protection. Finally, he reminds us that we have yet to find evidence of a cult of living kings among the Hittites.[42] On the other hand, there is the testimony of the Homeric poems with their epithets of the 'Zeus-born' type. One passage in the Odyssey is worth our attention, for it has often been compared with a passage in the Works and Days. In the nineteenth book of the Odyssey the hero of the poem pays Penelope a generous compliment, telling her that her glory is like that of the king who rules over many men, upholding the claims of justice. In sympathy the earth provides crops, the trees fruit, the animals young, and the sea fish, all as a consequence of the king's benevolent rule, and beneath his sway the people prosper (verses 108–14). We read in Hesiod how the people of the just city similarly flourish; peace reigns supreme and they experience no war, no famine, no disaster, but find joy in doing their work. The earth bears sustenance in plenty, the oak yields acorns and offers a home to the bees, their sheep are heavy with fleeces, and the women bear children who resemble their parents. In short, they have all they need without having to venture overseas in ships (verses 225–37). An earlier generation of scholars will tell us that the lines from the Odyssey are Hesiodic in substance and in style, but a moment's thought reveals the greater antiquity of the idea expressed by Homer.

That a good king leads to a good harvest is a common enough belief throughout the countries of the ancient Near East.[43] Although the Odyssey king is said to be god-fearing, there is no mention of Zeus or any other god, and it is rather a matter of the king working directly on nature without any god having to intervene; the king and nature function together in unison and no intermediary is necessary.[44] In Hesiod, however, the automatic response of nature has gone, and the presence of Zeus lurking in the clouds is always felt (verse 229, and later in the sketch of the unjust city, verses 239, 242, 245, and 247). Homer's king is personally responsible by his own good or bad deeds for the prosperity of his subjects, whereas Hesiod would have us believe that a single wicked man can bring disaster crashing down on his fellows (verses 240–1). According to Homer, such a degree of responsibility belongs to the king alone. A glance at the Plague Prayers of Mursilis reveals the same to have been true of the Hittite monarchs.[45] One can hardly expect a pharaoh to make a song and dance about his own shortcomings, but in the Instruction for Meri-ka-Re the king of Egypt goes as far as admitting his failings: Behold, a misfortune happened in my time. The Thinite regions were hacked up. It really happened through what I had done, and I knew of it only after it was done. Behold, my recompense came out of what I had done.[46] There is no reason why we should be bothered by the reference to the king's judicial duties in verse 111 of the Odyssey passage, for the administration of justice was among the king's most important functions in the Near East, while in the Iliad two of Agamemnon's three daughters bear the significant names of Chrysothemis and Laodike (ix, 145 and 287). A good idea of the duties of Pharaoh may be obtained by another look at the Instruction for Meri-ka-Re: Do justice whilst thou endurest upon earth. Quiet the weeper; do not oppress the widow; supplant no man in the property of his father; and impair no officials at their posts. Be on thy guard against punishing wrongfully. Do not slaughter: it is not of advantage to thee.[47] In the Ugaritic legend of Keret, when the king falls so dangerously ill as to be near death, his son and later his daughter can tell him that the valleys and a vast district weep and groan for him. At the end of the same story we are presented with another picture of a king's obligations towards his people, as Yassib invites his father to surrender the throne, claiming that in his failing strength Keret is not capable of judging the case of the widow and the wretched, of checking those who despoil the children of the poor, and of feeding the orphan and the widow.[48] From the evidence I have discussed I think it fair to conclude that the picture of the good king in the Odyssey reflects a tradition of considerable age, and, furthermore, a tradition which endows royalty with more than purely human powers.

If my second suggestion is accepted and it is agreed that the Greeks were directly influenced by Egypt, we are assuming that Hesiod owes something to Mycenaean tradition. The validity of the argument may be checked if we examine Hesiod's poetry to see whether we find other evidence in it of Mycenaean survivals. I have had to comment already on the Linear B tablets, and this new material may prove useful here also; it is of some help, though not free from uncertainties. The fact that the title *basileus* on the tablets appears to denote a provincial dignitary and a number of them is mentioned recalls Hesiod's use of the same word to describe the local princes of Boeotia. When Hesiod calls the carpenter the slave of Athene (Works and Days, 430), he is apparently using terminology derived from the Mycenaeans. On one tablet we may have a reference to 'Mother Theia', and so can compare Theogony, 135 and 371.[49] Most informative of all, a tablet from Knossos lists the offerings made to various deities, the first being Diktaian Zeus. Ventris and Chadwick illustrate the association of Zeus with Mount Dikte by a reference to Hesiod's story of the birth of the god.[50] Actually Hesiod does not mention Dikte, although nineteenth-century editors were apt to replace Lyktos in verse 482 by Dikte. What the poet says is that, when Rhea was on the point of giving birth to Zeus, she sought the advice of Gaia and Ouranos, who sent her to Lyktos in Crete. Gaia received Zeus in Crete, carried him to Lyktos, and hid him in a cave on Mount Aigaion (verses 468–84). Nilsson has discussed the identification of Hesiod's cave: because of the reference to Lyktos, Mount Aigaion must be Mount Lasithi, and the cave, therefore, should be either that of Psychro or that of Arkalochori. The cult centred in the first of these caves reached its climax in the Late Minoan period and ceased to be celebrated in the Geometric age. Arkalochori was sacred until the end of the Minoan era and Nilsson reports only 'a few doubtful Proto-geometric finds'.[51] Whether or not Hesiod really understood the geography of Crete, Nilsson is surely right when he affirms that the localization of the story must recall Minoan cult, as the caves of Mount Lasithi were later abandoned. The truth of his observation is strengthened by Hesiod's only other reference to Crete in the Theogony: according to Hesiod, Demeter, having joined in love with the hero Iasion, gave birth to Ploutos in fertile Crete (verses 969–71). The emphasis laid on the fertility of Crete and the suggestion of a *hieros gamos* provide further evidence of survivals from an age well before the Dorians overwhelmed Mycenaean Greece.[52]

I trust that I have now said enough to show that there is nothing improbable after all in the theory that Hesiod's description of the preparation of Pandora may be traced back to the Mycenaean period, and that, when we start to look for its origins, we must go beyond the confines of the Greek world. But there was also a second question to be investigated, the connection between the birth and coronation of a new king and the story of creation. The connection can best be seen if one glances at the songs of wild jubilation which greeted the accession of a new pharaoh in Egypt. In his introduction to the accession hymn of Mer-ne-Ptah, J. A. Wilson comments that 'in the dogma of Egyptian religion each pharaoh was a god who repeated the creation miracle of establishing order out of chaos'. The text of the hymn bears out his statement: Be glad of heart, the entire land! The goodly times are come! A lord – life, prosperity, health! – is given in all lands, and normality has come down again into its place: the King of Upper and Lower Egypt, the lord of millions of years, great of kingship like Horus: Ba-en-Re Meri-Amon – life, prosperity, health! – he who crushes Egypt with festivity, the Son of Re, most serviceable of any king: Mer-ne-Ptah Hotep-hir-Maat – life, prosperity, health! All ye righteous, come that ye may see! Right has banished wrong. Evildoers have fallen upon their faces. All the rapacious are ignored. The water stands and is not dried up; the Nile lifts high. Days are long, nights have hours, and the moon comes normally. The gods are satisfied and content of heart. One lives in laughter and wonder. Mayest thou know it.[53] Another hymn, this time one lauding the accession of Ramses IV, is of the same order: it describes the restoration of public confidence and prosperity, and how 'high Niles have come forth from their caverns' and ships can dispense with ropes 'for they come to land with wind and oars', that is to say, by taking advantage of the helpful current and breeze.[54]

The praise heaped upon the pharaoh's person in the hymns quoted is much more than the mere compliments required by convention. Egypt's first monarch was the Sun-god himself. Our sense of the passage of time was meaningless to the Egyptians, for whom change was possible only in the limited and recurrent pattern associated with the annual fall and rise of the Nile or the sun's daily journey through the heavens, its disappearance at nightfall, and its rebirth the following day. In spite of the many gods named as creators, the sun was regarded 'the primary source of creative energy'. Every pharaoh was a god like the first king of Egypt, and, while the pharaoh was distinct from Re, 'these two shared certain essential attributes'. Just as Re vanquished the dragon Apophis each night and was thus able to return to the sky the next morning, so, on ascending the throne, the pharaoh banished disorder and chaos from his realm and brought back normality once more. New Year's Day, or some other occasion which marked the revival of the forces of nature, was reserved for the coronation and *Sed* festival. Accession to the throne had to follow immediately upon the death of the previous king and could not be deferred until an appropriate day came along. But it was sunrise when accession occurred, 'so that there might be the propitious consonance between the beginning of the new reign and the start of the new day under the rulership of Re, the father and proto-type of kings'. The pharaoh is closely linked with Re, and 'the analogy with Re is stressed especially at the coronation, which can be regarded as the creation of a new epoch after a dangerous interruption of the harmony between society and nature – a situation, therefore, which partakes of the quality of the creation of the universe'.[55] This, I suggest, is the kind of connection which explains how the story told by the Deir el-Bahari reliefs could have become fused with a creation myth. The connection between the two survives as late as Hesiod, though the collapse of the Mycenaean civilization some four centuries before has caused it to lose its original significance.

I wish to return for a moment to texts discussed in the first two chapters of the book. At the beginning of our text of the Illuyanka myth (pp. 14–5), it is said that this story is the cult legend of the *Purulli* festival of the Storm-god. We know that Enuma Elish was recited in the course of the New Year festival at Babylon. The king played a pro-minent part in the proceedings of the festival: thus on the fifth day of the festival the king was brought before the statue of Marduk in the temple, stripped of his regalia, and struck on the cheek. He was then made to kneel before his god and delivered a confession in which he protested his innocence of any crime or act of negligence. Thereupon he had the royal insignia restored to him and received a second blow. If this drew tears, Marduk was well disposed and all would be favourable.[56] The relation of myth to ritual is a subject of considerable controversy into which I am reluctant to enter. Some, however, have argued that the Babylonian king was the god for the purposes of the festival, and that, as the god incarnate, he defeated Tiamat in a dramatic enactment of Enuma Elish; furthermore, it has been claimed that the festival was thought to represent the recreation of the universe and, at the same time, a repetition of the king's coronation. But this is speculation which, however interesting it may be, is incapable of proof. Yet in recent years the supreme importance of the king in cult has become increasingly clear. In the last chapter of *Myth, Ritual, and Kingship*, for example, Brandon, who delivers a devastating attack on the myth and ritual argument, singles out as a contribution of perman-ent value made by Hooke and his associates the fact that 'the exponents of the (myth and ritual) thesis have established beyond all doubt the

fundamental importance of kingship as a religious institution throughout the various cultures of the ancient Near East'.[57] When you begin
to think about the relation of myth to ritual, it is not difficult to let your
thoughts run wild. The point has been well made by a classical scholar,
Marlow, who has examined the evidence from early Greece in support
of the myth and ritual proposition. Although I share much of Marlow's
scepticism, I think it relevant to note that the possibility that ritual
lies at the back of epic poetry, including that of Homer, is now being
discussed. It should also be said that the Linear B tablets are beginning
to give us some idea of the ritual practices of the Mycenaean Greeks,
and a case has been presented for a Mycenaean version of the
Anthesteria and a New Year festival.[58]

But in the concluding part of chapter three I intend to follow an
altogether safer path, and shall commence by taking a brief look at
what the Egyptians had to say about the creation of the world.[59] The
first thing to strike one is the variety of creation stories current among
the Egyptians. Once more we have water, the primeval ocean Nun, at
the very beginning. A number of different gods could be thought the
creator, including gods we have already mentioned, such as Khnum,
Atum, and Amon, or some other deity, such as Ptah in the Memphite
Theology. The method of creation also varies: the technique of the
craftsman can be employed, or the gods may be produced by the power
of the divine word or by sexual act; they can also appear from an egg
or the primeval lotus flower. But I suggest that we follow the lead given
to us by Nilsson and concentrate on the separation of Geb and Nut by
the god Shu. According to this tradition Atum produced Shu and his
female counterpart Tefnut. They in turn were the parents of Geb, the
earth, here a male, and the female Nut, the sky. Heaven and earth
were separated when their father Shu raised Nut up from Geb. The
myth goes back to the third millennium B.C., as the Pyramid Texts refer
to the sequence Atum, Shu and Tefnut, and Nut (e.g. 1248 a–d and
5 c–d), and the separation of sky and earth (e.g. 1208 c), while Shu is
called 'Shu of Nut' (1992 a), an expression which Mercer calls a
breviloquence of 'Shu who supports Nut'.[60]

This in itself is interesting, but it becomes much more exciting when
we turn to a text which accompanies a picture of Shu supporting Nut
on part of the roof of the sarcophagus room in the cenotaph of Seti I
at Abydos; this structure dates around 1300 B.C. A large part of the
text is unintelligible, and it is only the first few lines which tell a clear
story. The text opens by saying that the stars sail to the end of the sky

on the outside of Nut at night and are visible, but they cannot be seen
during the day when they are inside Nut. After a couple of sentences,
the text continues: They enter her mouth in the place of her head in
the West. Then she ate them. Then Geb quarrelled with Nut, because
he was angry with her because of the eating of her young ones. Her
name was called 'Sow who eats her piglets,' because she ate them.
Then her father Shu lifted her and raised her to his head. He said:
Beware of Geb. Let him not quarrel with her because she eats their
children. She shall give birth to them and they shall live again, and
they shall come forth in the place at her hinder part in the East every
day, even as she gave birth the first time.[61] It is impossible to translate
the rest of the text. What can be read, however, proves the existence
in Egypt around 1300 B.C. of a tradition according to which the sky
devoured her own children. This resulted in a quarrel with her
husband, the earth, and they were separated. Nut, therefore, is comparable to Ouranos, inasmuch as they comprise the sky, and to Kronos,
another deity who swallowed his offspring. Such a conflation confirms
the view that the stories of the crimes committed by Ouranos and
Kronos are really two accounts of one and the same act. Even more
important is the possibility that here we may have isolated the source
of an incident in the Theogony for which we have otherwise no prototype, unless we count the very uncertain reference in the Kumarbi
myth (pp. 3–4 and 13–4). The motif of swallowing one's own children
is best explained in terms of Egyptian influence on the Theogony, and
so we have another example to add to Hesiod's description of the
preparation of Pandora.

A final Egyptian text helps us with the story of Pandora. This is the
story of the two brothers Anubis and Bata, which we know from a
manuscript dating about 1225 B.C. The brothers have divine names,
and the story appears to have a mythological background.[62] It begins
with the wife of Anubis falsely accusing Bata of assailing her virtue,
and Bata retiring to a place called the Valley of the Cedar where he
lived a life of solitude. Out of pity for the innocent, Re ordered Khnum
to fashion a wife for Bata, 'and Khnum made him a companion that
had fairer limbs than any woman in the whole land, and every god was
in her'. So far we have a myth where the main characters are a pair of
brothers, the gods are involved, and the supreme god causes the
craftsman god to fashion a woman of outstanding beauty as wife for
one of the brothers. Like Pandora, moreover, the woman was to be the
source of endless trouble. Bata was very much in love with his wife, but

the sea carried a lock of her hair off to Egypt. The smell of the lock was responsible for it being brought before Pharaoh, and wise men who were consulted announced that it belonged to a daughter of Re. A search for the woman was undertaken, and she eventually came to Egypt and became the wife of Pharaoh. She gave her new husband vital information which led to the death of Bata, who was brought back to life, however, by his brother Anubis. The woman made two further attempts to eliminate Bata but without success, and the story ends happily with Bata now king of Egypt. When we compare the Tale of the Two Brothers and Hesiod's story of Pandora, it is seen that events take by no means a similar course. At the same time, we do seem to detect in Hesiod echoes of this Egyptian story of a woman of great beauty, whom the god Re has Khnum produce to order. The main point to notice, I think, is that the Tale of the Two Brothers is pure myth like the story of Pandora, and we are no longer faced with an account of the birth of the pharaoh. In other words, it helps us to understand the transition from the Deir el-Bahari reliefs to Greek mythology.

Because the story of Pandora occurs in both the Theogony and the Works and Days, in this third chapter we have had to say much more about the latter poem by Hesiod. Almost inevitably we have been drawn to the subject of the next chapter, the Near East and the Works and Days. Our discussion of the Theogony has taught us what to expect, and so we may proceed more speedily. Unless we have been hopelessly wrong in our work so far, the Works and Days ought to offer some confirmation of the conclusions which are now beginning to emerge.

DIDACTIC LITERATURE IN GREECE AND THE NEAR EAST

So far we have been concentrating on Hesiod's Theogony. I now want to go on to examine the Works and Days along much the same lines, although my comments need not be developed to such lengths and one chapter should prove sufficient.[1] Our examination of the Near Eastern background of the Theogony has caused us to discuss a formidable list of Hittite, Ugaritic, Babylonian, and Egyptian texts, and we have seen the kind of thing which we must expect once we get down to the task of considering the comparative material. I also propose to say something in chapter four about the Homeric evidence, since this has recently been the subject of some speculation. In this way we shall be preparing ourselves for a general assessment of Hesiod's position in the development of Greek epic poetry. But before we come to that and related matters in the final chapter of the book, and before we collect the Near Eastern parallels which are our immediate concern, it will be necessary for us to consider the structure and contents of this other poem by Hesiod. By doing so, we shall clear the ground for a study of the comparative material.[2]

Hesiod opens the Works and Days by inviting the Muses of Pieria to sing of their father Zeus. It is Zeus who has the power to make or break men. The god is asked to keep a watch over the administration of justice, while Hesiod undertakes to instruct his brother Perses (verses 1–10). Although Pausanias (9, 31, 4) apparently saw a copy of the poem at Helicon inscribed on lead which omitted these verses, and they were therefore long under suspicion, few modern scholars would accept the authority of those dwelling around Helicon and commence the Works and Days with Hesiod's description of the two kinds of Strife. The poem has to have some sort of introduction, and I hope to show later that these verses are echoed by what Hesiod says at the end of the Works, when he discusses the dangers of Pheme. At verse 10 we make the transition from Zeus to what is to be the poet's main theme throughout the rest of his poem, reliable advice addressed in the first instance to the wretched Perses, but advice which certainly has an altogether wider application. If we compare, as we did in chapter three, Hesiod's two versions of the story of Prometheus and Pandora, we see that the Theogony never gets beyond the preparation of the first woman, whereas the Works and Days outlines the history of Pandora and her jar but hurries over the opening stages of the story, merely telling us that Zeus was furious because Prometheus had deceived him (verses 47–8). It seems reasonable to assume that Hesiod relies on his audience already knowing from the Theogony what happened in detail when the sacrifice was performed at Mekone, and that the Theogony, therefore, must be the earlier composition. Such a belief in the priority of the Theogony is confirmed right at the beginning of the Works and Days when Hesiod modifies what he says about the goddess Eris in the Theogony (verse 225) and substitutes for the single daughter of Night two contrasting types of Strife (verses 11–26). From the outset Hesiod establishes a relationship between family groups, first between the Muses and their father Zeus, then between Zeus, the father of men and gods, and mankind, and finally between two representatives of mankind, the brothers Hesiod and Perses. The next step in the process is another pair, the two Strifes, goddesses who correspond in disposition to the contrast between the characters of the two brothers. Hesiod's feeling for a balance in the universe between pairs of opposites continues to be expressed until the end of the poem, as we are constantly reminded of the antithesis between the strong and the weak, between what is right and what is wrong, between the ability to help and the ability to destroy.

By the time we have reached line 26 the nature of the good Eris has been fully explained: it is the spirit of competition which makes us all try to live up to the standard of our nextdoor neighbours, those ubiquitous Joneses. Hesiod then turns to her bad sister, the kind of Eris which fosters war and tumult and causes us to neglect our proper work, and this is identified with Perses' interest in litigation (cf. verses 14 and 33). After a cryptic reference to his quarrel with Perses, Hesiod passes via the proverb of verses 40–1 to the sad tale of yet another pair of vastly different character, the brothers Prometheus and Epimetheus, a story which really starts at verse 47 and ends at verse 105. There follows the myth of the ages, a part of the poem which, I would argue, ends at verse 173, when the life of the heroes, safely removed to the Isles of the Blessed, has been shown by verbal parallels to be identical to that enjoyed by the men of the golden age while still alive (cf. verses 111 and 169, 112 and 170, and 117–8 and 172–3). If we divide the poem in the way which I suggest, we find here both a perfect example of ring-composition and also a pattern, represented by the sequence good, bad, bad, good, which we see elsewhere in the description of the Erides (verses 12, 13, 14–6, and 17–26) and in the poet's later assessment of the relative merits of *dike* and *hybris* (verses 213, 213, 214–6, and 216–8), although in the second case the pattern is further developed by the pictures of the just and unjust cities to yield a sequence of the ABBAAB type.[3]

The subject under discussion from line 174 on is justice, and then, after 297, work. In the first of these two sections of the Works and Days we meet Hesiod's description of the age of iron (verses 174–201), the fable of the hawk and the nightingale (verses 202–12), and the contrast between *dike* and *hybris*, the last, as I pointed out above, being further developed by the descriptions of the just and unjust cities (verses 225–37 and 238–47). Then the kings are addressed and reminded of their moral obligations, for thirty thousand spirits range the earth looking after justice, a royal privilege given to the men of the golden age when translated from earth (cf. verses 121–6 and 252–5). Next we begin to hear of Perses again (verses 274 ff.), and that brings us back to the commencement of the poem and the question of work (cf. especially 21–4 and 312–3, and 5–7 and 325 and 379). Perses is told about his social obligations and his duty towards the gods, and this is followed by more instructions on how to order our lives in relation to our fellows and by practical advice on the subject of women and the family. Verses 383–617 comprise a calendar, although not without digressions, of the year's work on the farm. It opens and closes with a reference to the Pleiades (verses 383–4 and 614–6) and a direct appeal to Perses (verses 397 and 611), which thus mark off the limits of the compositional ring. Seafaring can be a useful supplement to farming and, as early as line 45 (cf. verse 629), received a brief acknowledgement. Another reference to the Pleiades and Orion (cf. verses 572, 598, 609, 615, and 619) introduces us to Hesiod on the sea and its perils. Then we return to the advice which was interrupted by the farmer's calendar and read more about marriage (verses 695 ff.). Next comes a list of prohibitions, most of which are dictated by religious scruples (verses 707 ff.), before the Works is brought to a close by lines warning us of the dangers of Pheme (verses 760–4). Finally, we have the Days.

The Works and Days is far from being the amorphous shambles that some believe it to be. The clue to its structure, in my opinion, is to be found in Hesiod's exploitation of the principle of ring-composition. By using this device to stamp the beginning and end of sections within his poem, Hesiod was able to marshal and reduce to a system what at a cursory glance appears an imperfectly digested collection of rambling information. Furthermore, the poet's employment of ring-composition goes considerably beyond a repetition of word or phrase and the expression of parallel sentiments. Thus the beginning and end of the Works are linked tightly together as the only places in the poem where Hesiod adds to the gods and goddesses of the Theogony. We commence with a good Eris to match the bad Eris of the Theogony, and conclude by reading that Pheme also ranks as something divine. This is Hesiod's most daring attempt to use ring-composition, since it provides the extreme limits of the Works within which all the other smaller rings must be fitted. At the same time, in the case of the Erides and Pheme, it is not just words that are echoed, but it is even possible to see the same process of thought at work in Hesiod's mind. I used to believe that both the Days and the introductory verses dedicated to the omnipotence of Zeus lay outside the bounds of this main ring, but now I am inclined to argue that it is the *prooemium* plus the description of the Strifes which balances the deification of Pheme. The single Eris in the Theogony prepares the way for the two Erides of the Works, and the two Erides, taken in conjunction with the opening eulogy of Zeus, anticipate Hesiod's remarks about the terrible power of Pheme, which, accordingly, do much more than simply pick up the advice offered in verses 715–21. Zeus remains in the forefront of Hesiod's mind even when he tells us to avoid men's talk.

The *prooemium* bears witness to the power of Zeus: Hymn Zeus, Muses, through whom men are famed or unfamed, sung or unsung, as Zeus directs (verses 1–4). Verses 3 and 4, and 5 and 6 form pairs of couplets with the second two telling of Zeus' ability to humble the mighty and exalt the weak. Verses 5, 6, and 7 all begin with the same adverb, but verse 7 stands apart from the others, since it strikes for the first time a moral note and no longer opposes two groups, the strong and the weak, but, by referring to the crooked and the arrogant, gives an expansion of ideas and not a contrast.[4] In verses 3 and 4 a man's greatness or lack of greatness is made to consist of his fame. One thinks at once of Homer's heroes who regard public opinion with such awe. In any society where there is little or no belief in life after death a reputation kept alive by subsequent generations provides the solitary hope of any form of permanent survival. The Romans, equally obsessed with the idea of *gloria*, were anxious to leave behind them some tangible evidence of their achievements on this earth. But Hesiod's code of morality is not the same as that of Homer, for, while Homer would revel in the brutal hawk, all of Hesiod's sympathies are with the helpless nightingale. Does Hesiod, then, regard reputation in the same way as Homer? When we look at verses 3 and 4, the answer appears to be a firm negative, for, as Verdenius has indicated, Hesiod modifies the Homeric concept of reputation. Reputation no longer depends on men and on what they may care to say. It is now 'through Zeus' and 'at Zeus' direction' that men are celebrated or obscure, and it is the god, and not men, that we must think of as bestowing a fair or sordid reputation.

Hesiod returns to the problem of reputation when, in the closing lines of the Works, he completes his main ring. The succession of adjectives and infinitives in verses 761–2 and the adverb ῥεῖα at the beginning of verse 762 achieve the same effect as that we have seen in the case of verses 3 to 6. But reputation in the Pheme passage is certainly associated with men, for Hesiod advises us to avoid 'the terrible talk of men' and claims that 'talk never entirely perishes whenever many people repeat it'. But the second half of verse 764, where Pheme is said to be divine, may resolve the contradiction; perhaps Pheme qualifies as a deity not only because men keep it alive by their constant chatter, but also because it is something intimately connected with father Zeus. In the following line the days are said to come from Zeus, and so too, according to the opening verses of the poem, does reputation. It is difficult to resist the temptation of reading between the lines and coming out in support of two kinds of Pheme, one originating with Zeus and the other an inferior version bestowed by mankind, but this would be as dangerous as Pheme herself. Yet it cannot be without significance that the idea of reputation occurs both at the beginning and at the close of the Works, just as it is significant that here alone Hesiod is ready to add new deities to the already large pantheon of the Greeks.

In discussing the structure of the Works and Days I have inevitably had to say much about the contents of the poem. Throughout its entire length Hesiod is anxious to provide his brother Perses with sound moral and practical advice, and advice, moreover, from which all men can profit equally. I should like to believe that Hesiod was the elder of the two brothers, but there is only one piece of evidence to support an impression that this must be true. The good Eris is said to have been born before her bad sister (verse 17), and, while it is possible that priority of birth merely implies superiority (cf. Iliad xiii, 355 and Odyssey xix, 184), this may mean that Hesiod as a living representative of the good spirit of competition, compared to Perses who equals the bad Eris, was also the first born. Of course, Hesiod is prepared to do more than offer sound advice; he is, in addition, willing to advance explanations. Thus we have the myth of Prometheus and the story of the ages of mankind. A Near Eastern origin has been suggested for both episodes. It is easy to think of Pandora as the Greek equivalent of Eve, for both ladies illustrate the risks that man faces in his relations with the other sex. Also important is the idea that the gods want to deny to mortals the essentials of civilized life, but these are obtained through the intervention of a third party. Such a theme provides the plot of a Sumerian myth which relates how Inanna, the goddess of Erech, was able to persuade the god Enki to surrender to her the divine laws which form the basis of civilized life.[5] The goddess, eager to promote the prosperity and fame of her own city and its inhabitants, achieved her purpose by making Enki drunk. But once he had recovered, Enki regretted his generosity and despatched his messenger Isimud, accompanied by sea monsters, in an attempt to stop the boat on which Inanna, having loaded the divine laws, was making her way back to Erech. In spite of several attacks, Inanna's own vizier, the god Ninshubur, saved the craft and its precious cargo. Eventually it reached Erech where the divine laws were safely landed.

The source of the myth of the ages remains a great problem. It is certainly possible that we should seek its origin in the countries of the Near East, but Martin Nilsson, a scholar whose opinion is highly respected, has been consistently opposed to the suggestion, and as yet we have no really convincing analogy. But we do know of a Sumerian poem in which silver and mighty copper argue their respective merits, and this can be supplemented with other scraps of evidence, all, however, too late in date to be of much relevance.[6] Although we cannot isolate its origin, it is possible to see one stage in the evolution of the myth of the ages in the addition of the fifth age, that of iron, by Hesiod himself. Hesiod's descriptions of the first four ages culminate in an account of what happened to their members after they had died. Since it adds nothing to the myth in its present context, this may reflect the purpose served by the myth in a pre-Hesiodic form.[7] We learn nothing about the fate after death of the iron age men, because it was added by the poet to fit his particular use of the myth. The choice of iron to characterize his own age was clearly determined by the prevalence of this metal in the society familiar to Hesiod (cf. verses 387, 420, and 743). But apart from saying this, all one can do is to guess. Verses 150–1 read rather strangely not only because of their reference to bronze houses, but also because of the abrupt fashion in which it is stated that 'there was no black iron'. The prior existence of an era when bronze was the chief metal in use could easily have been deduced from the anachronizing of epic poetry or the survival of bronze implements in ritual. The myth of the ages, on the other hand, may well go back to the bronze age. A belief in a past age of perfection is a common enough concept and could have arisen independently of any series of metallic ages. The heroes have obviously been introduced into the scheme in order to relate so important a group to the other ages of mankind.

The Near East does not help us at the moment with the myth of the ages. Nevertheless, it has a great deal to contribute to our understanding of the Works and Days in other respects. The group of texts from the Near East to be compared with Hesiod's poem is that which consists of the instruction type of wisdom text where one person advises another on how to conduct himself and how to regulate his life and behaviour. Egypt offers the best examples, and these cover an immense stretch of time, extending from the period of the Old Kingdom in the third millennium B.C. to a date later than Hesiod.[8] Much of the advice set forth is of a standard kind, and different texts, widely separated in time, include the same moral and practical axioms. The earliest of them of which we possess the full text, the Instruction of Ptah-hotep, is characteristic. In it one learns of the need to listen to others, to be impartial, to refrain from slander, to be generous and not greedy. We are told that, although fraud may bring riches, it is justice which lasts. Practical advice includes instructions on how to handle various people.[9] The person offering the advice is a father and the one being instructed his son. Ptah-hotep was vizier to King Izezi of the fifth dynasty, but neither the adviser nor the advised has to occupy a particularly exalted social position, so that in the Instruction of Ani the parent is just a scribe. But the two texts most relevant to a study of the Works and Days are the Instruction of Amen-em-Opet and the Instructions of 'Onchsheshonqy. Neither text is easy to date with any degree of precision, but the original composition of the former must surely be considerably earlier than Hesiod, while the other appears to be later and may reflect the influence of the Works and Days. Another wisdom text, which serves to bridge the gap between the two documents just mentioned, has recently been identified; one waits impatiently for the full publication of this work, but already we know that it has advice to offer the farmer not unlike that associated with Hesiod's poem.[10]

Parallel passages in the Instruction of Amen-em-Opet and the Book of Proverbs have been much discussed, and at long last the priority of the Egyptian text seems settled. But a link with Hesiod appears just as evident when, in chapter six of the thirty chapters in which the Instruction of Amen-em-Opet is arranged, we come across the following passage (cf. Works and Days, 298 ff. and 320 ff.):

> Cultivate the fields, that thou mayest find what thou needest;
> and receive the bread of thine own threshing-floor;
> better is a bushel that God giveth thee
> than five thousand obtained by force;
> they stay not a day in store and barn,
> they make no food in the beer-jar;
> a moment is their duration in the granary,
> when morning cometh they have gone below.[11]

The text continues (cf. verses 40–1):

> Better is poverty at the hand of God
> than riches in the storehouse;
> better is bread with happy heart
> than riches with vexation.

The twenty-fifth chapter includes this comment (cf. verses 5–8):

> Verily man is clay and straw,
> God is his fashioner;
> he pulls down and builds up each day.

Here we may have evidence for an Egyptian belief that clay was the ingredient from which mankind was formed (pp. 64–5), but more important for the present is the similarity between the idea expressed in this passage and Hesiod's personal concept of the power of Zeus. Although I shall content myself with these three examples, it should be noticed that much of the other advice presented by Pharaoh's overseer of the land and grains recalls the words of the Greek poet.

In his edition of the Instructions of 'Onchsheshonqy Glanville points out that this work differs from other Egyptian wisdom texts in a number of respects.[12] The morality it recommends can be both elevated and also inspired by unadulterated self-interest. Its contents suggest that it was addressed to an audience of peasant farmers, while its author reveals a deep understanding of country life and shows himself to be well acquainted with its lore. Glanville can claim that 'again and again his images are taken from the farm or from nature – to a degree which is perhaps unique in Egyptian literature of any kind'.[13] Those features which distinguish the Instructions of 'Onchsheshonqy and set it in a class of its own among the Egyptian wisdom texts are also to be found in the Works and Days, and I have, therefore, argued as a working hypothesis that we ought to consider the possibility that it is Hesiod here who influences Egyptian literature rather than the reverse.[14] Passage after passage from Hesiod may be set beside an extract from the Instructions of 'Onchsheshonqy where we find the identical sentiment expressed, and the accumulation of parallels which results is most impressive. Whichever way the influence flowed, that one text did influence the other seems beyond dispute.

But there is something else rather special about the Instructions of 'Onchsheshonqy which we shall find it worth our while to discuss. The instructions themselves are preceded by an introduction occupying five out of the twenty-seven and a half columns of the text, where we have a story which explains how 'Onchsheshonqy came to compile advice for the benefit of his son. It seems that he was involved in a conspiracy against Pharaoh when Pharaoh preferred to consult a younger brother rather than the elder son who had succeeded his father as court physician. This slight constituted an affront to all holders of high office, and a conspiracy was hatched. The plot was discovered by Pharaoh, and 'Onchsheshonqy, who knew of it but had not reported it, was cast into prison, from where he wrote his instructions. Glanville calls the story pseudo-history, for, while the pharaoh himself is unnamed, others are mentioned by name and there is a reference to the accession anniversary.[15] A dispute between brothers sets the conspiracy in motion, and it is not surprising that we find among the instructions pieces of advice of the following kind: Oh may the kindly brother of the family be the one who acts as 'elder brother' for it! (10, 15); Do not go to your brother if you are in trouble; go to your friend (16, 4); Better to be without a brother than to have a brother who is evil (21, 21). Hesiod, I imagine, would have heartily endorsed such words of wisdom, but more interesting is the fact that both in Hesiod and the Egyptian didactic text a story is attached to the instructions. The same combination of narrative and advice is also used in another text, again one of late date, which we may now go on to consider.

We know the names of several Egyptian wise men. Thus the work known as 'In Praise of Learned Scribes' ends: Is there anyone here like Hor-dedef? Is there another like Ii-em-hotep? None has appeared among our relatives like Neferti or Khety, that foremost of them. I cause thee to know the names of Ptah-em-Djedhuti and Kha-kheper-Re-seneb. Is there another like Ptah-hotep, or Ka-iris as well? These learned men who foretold what was to come, that which issued from their mouths happened, being found as a statement written in their books. Thus the children of other people are given to them to be heirs, as though they were their own children. Though they concealed their magic from everyone else, it may be read in a book of wisdom. Though they are gone and their names are forgotten, it is writing that makes them remembered.[16]

The same tradition of the wise man is to be seen further to the East, where it is best exemplified by the Words of Ahiqar.[17] Our earliest text of the work dates from the late fifth century B.C. and is written in Aramaic. The first four of its eleven papyrus sheets tell in the first person the story of Ahiqar, while the advice of Ahiqar covers the remaining seven. The narrative part of the text tells how Ahiqar, having grown old in the service of the Assyrian king Sennacherib and having no son of his own, adopted a nephew and got the new king Esarhaddon to appoint the nephew his successor. But the nephew played Ahiqar false, and Esarhaddon ordered the old man's death. The officer sent to carry out the execution, in return for a similar service to himself in the past, only pretended to do as he had been instructed, and concealed Ahiqar while announcing his death. The end of the story is missing, but we know from later versions of it that the king subsequently regretted his rashness in believing the nephew's accusations and was overjoyed to learn that Ahiqar still lived. Ahiqar was accordingly restored to the royal favour, while the treacherous nephew was suitably punished. Although this story is set in the reigns of Sennacherib and Esarhaddon of Assyria, who occupied the throne in the first half of the seventh century B.C., concealment in order to escape disaster is a common theme, examples of which are to be seen in the Iliad (vi, 135–7 and xviii, 394–405). It is true that we have no direct prototype of the complete story of Ahiqar, but we can trace back in our Babylonian texts the theme of the minister who is disgraced only to be later restored to office, and it is possible that this had already been combined with the theme of the ungrateful nephew.[18]

The actual sayings of Ahiqar take some time telling us how to handle the king, and such advice is presumably intended for a person like Ahiqar's successor, who would be likely to be in contact with royalty. In giving his advice, Ahiqar makes use of the fable. and we hear about the leopard and the goat, the bear and the lambs, and the bramble and the pomegranate tree. One of the best known passages in the Works and Days is Hesiod's fable of the hawk and the nightingale (verses 202–12), and, while this may be the first animal fable in Greek literature, it is far from being the earliest fable preserved. Recent years have witnessed the publication of more and more Sumerian fables, and although so far we have no fable which exactly parallels Hesiod's story of the hawk and the nightingale, Sumerian fables are known which echo the spirit of Hesiod's own.[19] Two examples will make my point clear: The lion had caught a 'bush'-pig and proceeded to bite him, saying, 'Until now, your flesh has not filled my mouth, but your squeals have created a din in my ears!' (5, 57); The pork-butcher slaughters the pig, saying, 'Must you squeal? This is the road which your sire and your grand-sire travelled, and now you are going on it too! And yet you are squealing!' (8, 2).

We also have evidence for the instruction type of literature among the Babylonians. Thus a series of warnings addressed to a king occurs on a tablet unearthed from the libraries of Ashurbanipal. The king and, at the end of the tablet, his officers are warned of the divine retribution which lies in wait for the oppressor of the citizens of Sippar, Nippur, and Babylon.[20] It is not possible to link the text with any one king, and all we can say is that a king of Babylon between 1000 and 700 B.C. would be a suitable recipient of the warnings. The style adopted is that of an omen text, and each warning consists of a protasis 'if something or other is done or not done' (cf. Works and Days, 327 ff.), followed by a statement of the appropriate disaster which will ensue. More revealing is the Instructions of Shuruppak, a work of Sumerian origin of which we possess a scrap of a Babylonian translation; the Sumerian original is over three hundred lines long, but very little has been published to date.[21] We know from the introduction that Shuruppak delivered his advice to a son named Ziusudra. The latter was the hero of the Sumerian flood story, and perhaps the Instructions of Shuruppak is to be connected with the catastrophe, for the flood was the result of man's crime, and advice was required if a repetition of the tragedy was to be avoided for the future. Texts discovered at Ugarit have established the influence of Babylonian wisdom literature outside Mesopotamia itself. One, an Akkado-Hurrian bilingual, reinforces my remarks in chapter one (pp. 19–21) about the importance of the Hurrians as middlemen. A much longer text of Babylonian origin, where a father addresses his son who seems from the first instructions to be on the point of leaving the family home, was recovered from a private house at Ugarit during 1959, and more texts have since been discovered.[22]

It has been erroneously suggested that the Instructions of Shuruppak might supply the missing beginning of the Babylonian text usually called the Counsels of Wisdom.[23] This document is an obvious one for us to discuss next, since it is a composition of some one hundred and sixty lines offering moral advice. Variations in metre and contents cause Lambert to divide the poem into the following sections, each of which deals with a separate topic: avoidance of bad companions; improper speech; avoidance of altercations and pacification of enemies; kindness to those in need; the undesirability of marrying a slave girl; the unsuitability of prostitutes as wives; the temptations of a vizier; improper speech; the duties and benefits of religion; and deception of friends. The section for which there is no corresponding advice offered by Hesiod is that on the temptations to which a vizier is exposed. Unlike the rest of the Counsels of Wisdom, this part of the text has a specific rather than a general relevance, and it begins, moreover, with the address 'my son'. These facts suggest that the collection of precepts was delivered by a vizier to the son destined to succeed him in that capacity, and that the work, therefore, may fall into the same category as the Words of Ahiqar. It is not easy to determine when the Counsels of Wisdom was originally composed, but Lambert opts for the Cassite period (1500–1200 B.C.).

Hesiod is very keen that Perses should get on with his proper work and not waste time hanging around the law court (verses 27 ff.). The beginnings of three lines of the Babylonian translation of the Instructions of Shuruppak refer to a dispute. A clearer picture of what the Babylonians thought to be the best course of action if one was involved in litigation can be gained from the third section of the Counsels of Wisdom. There the person receiving instruction is told not to frequent the law court and linger where there is a dispute. 'When confronted with a dispute, go your way; pay no attention to it. Should it be a dispute of your own, extinguish the flame!' (36–7). Improper speech is another subject on which Hesiod held strong views. The second discussion of this topic in the Counsels of Wisdom is worth quoting in full, because it ties in well with Hesiod's comments on the dangers of Pheme:

> Do not utter libel, speak what is of good report.
> Do not say evil things, speak well of people.
> One who utters libel and speaks evil,

men will waylay him with his debit account to Shamash.
Beware of careless talk, guard your lips;
do not utter solemn oaths while alone,
for what you say in a moment will follow you afterwards.
But exert yourself to restrain your speech (127–34).

Shamash, the god mentioned in the passage which I have quoted, was the Babylonian Sun-god, and the fact that the sun appears to watch over all men and their deeds made Shamash as well the god of justice, who, according to a long hymn of two hundred lines, 'determine(s) the lawsuit of the wronged' (127).[24] Shamash is depicted commissioning Hammurabi to draw up his code of laws on the stele on which our copy of the code is inscribed.

The idea that the Sun-god has this dual function helps us to interpret a puzzling reference in the Works and Days where Hesiod says that the all seeing and all perceiving eye of Zeus, if it is so inclined, looks down on the kind of justice a city practises (verses 267–9). Other allusions make it very probable that by the eye of Zeus Hesiod meant the sun.[25] Thus Homer refers to Helios 'who sees all and hears all' (Iliad iii, 277, and Odyssey xi, 109 and xii, 323), and it is Helios who sees Ares and Aphrodite at their play and carries a report to the husband Hephaistos (Odyssey viii, 270–1 and 302). In this passage from the Works and Days, therefore, it is likely that the sun acts as a god of justice on the pattern of the Mesopotamian and Hittite Sun-gods, although elsewhere in the poem this is the prerogative of either Zeus or his daughter Dike. The sacred number of Shamash was twenty, and it was on the twentieth day of the month that the Babylonians celebrated the festival of Shamash. Thus we read in the Hymn to Shamash:

On the twentieth day you exult with mirth and joy,
you eat, you drink their pure ale, the barman's beer
                                        from the market.

They pour out the barman's beer for you, and you accept (156–8).
In the Days Hesiod has something to say about the twentieth of the month: that is the day for the birth of a truly clever child (verses 792–3). Perhaps, if we press the meaning of the word ἴστωρ (cf. Iliad xviii, 501 and xxiii, 486), it may be argued that the cleverness of such a child consists of an ability to give a fair decision. That the twentieth was Shamash's day can explain why Hesiod tells us this about the character of a person born on that day of the month, especially as the sixth is the only day otherwise on which he makes a similar comment

(verses 788–9). If, furthermore, the poet has a particular brand of wisdom in mind, that of the judge, then a connection with Shamash ceases to be merely possible and may even be thought very likely.

When a comparative study is attempted, it is always a problem to decide how widely one ought to cast the net. The literature of Egypt at the time of the First Intermediate Period strikes much the same note as the Works and Days because of its preoccupation with disaster and its deep pessimism. These characteristics are to be seen repeatedly in the various Prophecies, the Dispute over Suicide, and the Story of the Eloquent Peasant. The last named is interesting as there already we have a text which may be regarded as a pure story or 'equally well . . as a discourse on equity with a narrative setting'.[26] Thus we find the same mixture of narrative and advice as we noted in the Works and Days, the Instructions of 'Onchsheshonqy, and the Words of Ahiqar, all three of which are much later in date. Egyptian hymns where a worshipper appeals for help in the law court suggest Hesiod's own dilemma. Babylonian hymns afford many opportunities for moral judgments to be made, and one of these, the Hymn to Shamash, has been discussed above. But there is in addition one other instruction text, and this I have deliberately left to the end, for it provides us with a Near Eastern equivalent of Hesiod's farmer's calendar, and it is agricultural instruction that one tends to associate with the poet from Ascra.

In chapter two (p. 39) I mentioned that the dragon slayer *par excellence* in Mesopotamian tradition was the god Ninurta. A Sumerian myth describes how the god defeated the demon Asag, although only after first fleeing 'like a bird'.[27] But the defeat of Asag was followed by the waters of the Kur or underworld, where Asag had had his abode, rising to the surface and preventing fresh water from reaching the fields. The situation was desperate until Ninurta piled stones over the Kur, heaping them up to form a great wall in front of Sumer. This checked the rise of the waters of the Kur, and the flood already covering the land was led into the Tigris by Ninurta. As a result

> Behold, now, everything on earth,
> rejoiced afar at Ninurta, the king of the land,
> the fields produced abundant grain,
> the vineyard and orchard bore their fruit,
> the harvest was heaped up in granaries and hills,
> the lord made mourning to disappear from the land,
> he made happy the spirit of the gods.

Ninurta also appears in the Sumerian farmers' almanac, a text which is comprised of a one-line introduction, 'In days of yore a farmer instructed his son', one hundred and seven lines of advice, and a colophon of three lines where the instructions are said to be those of Ninurta, trustworthy farmer of Enlil.[28] A provisional translation of the text enables us to follow a full year's activities on the Sumerian farm, starting with the inundation of the fields in May-June and finishing twelve months later when the crops, newly harvested, have to be winnowed and cleaned.

The almanac commences with advice on irrigation procedure and the preparation of the soil. The latter is complicated: once the water has been emptied from the field, oxen with their hooves protected are to trample the soil, stripping it of weeds, and making it level; the surface is then to be dressed with light axes, the marks left by the hooves of the oxen are to be eliminated by the use of pickaxes, and all the crevices worked over with a drag (2–12). While the field is left to dry out, the farm tools, including whips to supply an added incentive to the labourers, must be made ready (13–21). The farmer is recommended to operate his plough with two oxen, for 'sustenance is in a plough!' Next we are told to have the ground ploughed twice with two different sorts of plough each time, harrowed and raked three times, and, after that, pulverized with a hammer. 'Let the handle of your whip uphold you; brook no idleness. Stand over them during their work, and brook no interruptions. Do not distract your field workers. Since they must carry on by day and by heaven's stars for ten days, their strength should be spent on the field, and they are not to dance attendance on you' (22–40). Ploughing and sowing formed a single operation, a seeder being attached to the plough. The farmer learns how many furrows to plough and how much barley seed to sow per strip, and receives detailed advice on the type of furrow which he is to employ. If the barley is to sprout successfully, all clods must be removed, and any irregularity in the level treated (41–63).

We now turn from the care of the soil to the care of the barley crop itself. When the barley first begins to break the surface, two things are necessary, to address a prayer to Ninkilim, the goddess of field mice and vermin, and to frighten away the birds. The barley has to be watered at various stages in its growth. If the watered barley turns red, it is diseased, but if it is doing well, an extra ration of water will increase its yield by ten per cent (64–72). A team of three, a reaper, a binder, and someone to set up the sheaves, should do the job of harvesting. The farmer is urged to be charitable and leave the fallen kernels on the ground, so that the needy can pick them up; by doing this, the farmer will ensure the everlasting favour of his god (73–86). After harvesting come threshing and winnowing, and the first essential is to have the threshing-floor made level and the bins prepared. Threshing is to be carried out by having wagons drawn back and forth over the mounds of barley for a period of five days and by the use of threshing sledges (87–99). When the barley is winnowed, two men are to act as lifters. Prayers should be said when the barley is heaped up and on the evening and night of the day on which it is to be cleaned (100–8). 'These are the instructions of Ninurta, the son of Enlil. O Ninurta, trustworthy farmer of Enlil, your praise is good!' (109–11)

Kramer points out that it was no simple farmer who composed this almanac of work on the farm. Its author almost certainly was a professor at a Sumerian school, and it was intended to teach the technique of farming, thus enabling a graduate from a Sumerian school to find himself employment as the manager of a large estate; indeed we have a Sumerian essay where an argument takes place between two such graduates, one the scribe on an estate and the other its *ugula* (probably superintendent).[29] This suggests why the Sumerian text is much more prosaic than the farmer's calendar by Hesiod and has nothing remotely comparable to the descriptions of winter and summer in the Works and Days (verses 504–63 and 582–96). The type of agriculture practised in the East differs from that to be found in Greece to an appreciable extent, and this difference is reflected by the two calendars. Yet, at the same time, if we compare our Sumerian and Greek texts, they share more than just the basic scheme of a year's agricultural work discussed in chronological order. Hesiod tells us to pray to Zeus Chthonios and Demeter as we start ploughing (verses 465–9), and at several points in the Instructions of Ninurta the Sumerian farmer is advised to pray. But this, I suppose, is what we may expect of the early agriculturalist and, taken by itself, does not add up to very much. Hesiod warns us to take precautions to prevent the birds eating the seeds (verses 469–71) and would have us sweep the cobwebs from our containers (verse 475), but these perhaps are obvious pieces of advice. More significant is the fact that both texts appreciate the need to have the farm implements in serviceable shape. Hesiod's list includes the mortar and pestle, a mallet, and plough (verses 423 ff.), and, like his Sumerian counterpart, Hesiod believes that we should have a yoke of oxen to draw the plough (verses 436–8).

But surely the Sumerian calendar is discussing the management of a large estate, whereas Hesiod's farmer has very little to call his own? It is true that one is apt to think of Hesiod as a member of a depressed farming community, as if the population of Boeotia was divided into only two distinct groups, the rich nobility and a downtrodden peasantry. Yet a century later in Attica, at the time when Solon undertook his economic reforms, the state consisted of four classes, the pentakosiomedimnoi, hippeis, zeugitai, and thetes, and the limit separating the second and third classes was just one hundred measures. If a similar classification were to be applied to Hesiod, in which of these four categories should we have to place the poet? On the one hand, the farmer might have to try and borrow oxen and a wagon, but only if he had been neglectful (verses 452–4). On the other, he does not work alone: it seems that he can hire the assistance of a friend (verse 370), owns an establishment which includes a female servant and a plough ox (verses 405–7), and has mules at his disposal (verse 607). There are others to help on the farm, a lively fellow of forty to direct the plough (verses 441–5), and a little boy to hide the seed from the birds (verses 469–71). The farmer must join his hands in the toil (verses 458–61), but he does at least have hands to share in his work (cf. verses 502, 573, 597, 608, and 766). He is not said to whip the labourers, but his attitude is no more sentimental than that of the Sumerian farmer, for Hesiod coldbloodedly suggests that, when threshing is completed, we get rid of the male help and replace him with a childless female (verses 600–3).[30]

. The distance from Nippur and Ur, places where very important texts of the farmers' almanac have been discovered, to Greece is considerable, as is the length of time, some thousand years, which separates the Sumerian calendar from Hesiod's enumeration of the work of the farmer. It would be helpful if so large a gap, both geographical and chronological, could be bridged, but I can offer only one clue and that clue, I must admit, is an elusive one. We know that the Senate of Rome was so impressed with the agricultural skill of the Carthaginians that it had the twenty-eight volumes of Mago of Carthage, 'the father of agriculture' according to Columella, translated into Latin. The Carthaginians apparently, by developing the agricultural resources of North Africa to a high degree, acquired among the Romans a massive reputation for this science. This in turn suggests the skill of the native Phoenicians and makes Syria the centre of a lively interest in agricultural techniques. But the solitary piece of evidence I can quote in this connection is the brief calendar of farming activities to be found inscribed on the limestone plaque recovered at Gezer in Palestine, which seems to date from the second half of the tenth century B.C.[31]

We have now completed our survey of the different texts from Egypt and Mesopotamia in which one person gives another the benefit of his superior knowledge and experience. Homer's characters can do the same thing, and so we have passages in the Iliad which fall into the instruction category, the best example being offered in the ninth book of the Iliad, where Phoenix joins in trying to persuade Achilles to fight again. Phoenix is not Achilles' father, but he is the person on whose knees the infant Achilles sat and took food. Peleus treated Phoenix like an only son, and Phoenix made up for his own lack of offspring by treating Peleus' son as if Achilles were his own flesh and blood (verses 480–95). When Achilles joined Agamemnon, Phoenix went with the hero to teach him to be a speaker of words and a doer of deeds (verses 438–43). In his effort to soften the heart of Achilles, Phoenix gives an account of the events which drove him into exile, and the digression is developed at some length (verses 447 ff.). We learn of the quarrel with his father and the curse which meant that he could have no children of his own. His statement that even the gods are open to persuasion leads on to his description of the Litai, who, like Dike, are the daughters of Zeus, and the pernicious Ate (verses 497–514). Finally, he strengthens his argument that Achilles should receive the overtures of Agamemnon by relating, again at length, the story of Meleager, where the curse theme reappears (verses 529–99).[32]

But Achilles remains adamant, and we must wait until book nineteen before Achilles and Agamemnon are reconciled. When Agamemnon replies to Achilles, we hear once more about Ate, also a daughter of Zeus, who is capable of blinding the mind of even her father (verses 86 ff.). He illustrates his words by relating how Hera tricked Zeus into making Eurystheus and not Heracles lord of Argos (verses 95–133). Achilles is now so furious for battle that he will not wait to take his gifts, and Odysseus has to intervene with the suggestion that the troops be fed before they march against the foe (verses 154 ff.). Achilles will have none of this, but Odysseus has the last word, claiming that his greater age implies a greater degree of knowledge; Odysseus' seniority is made clear later when Antilochos says that he belongs to an earlier generation (xxiii, 790). Practical advice as well as moral exhortation can be offered to Homer's heroes: thus Nestor instructs his son Antilochos before the chariot race at the funeral games of Patroclos. Superior technique can compensate for the relative slowness of

Antilochos' horses, for it is by skill, so Nestor claims, that the wood-
cutter, pilot, and charioteer excel. Provided that his advice is followed
at the turn in the course, nobody will be able to overtake Antilochos,
even if he should be driving Arion, the horse of Adrastos, or those of
Laomedon (xxiii, 304–48). Finally, it will be remembered how Achilles,
in an attempt to check the grief of Priam, refers to the pithoi of Zeus
(xxiv, 527 ff.) and later quotes the experience of Niobe (verses 602 ff.).

Others have compared these passages with Hesiod's technique in the
Works and Days.[33] I, however, wish to emphasize a difference, the
seniority of the person who offers an opinion. In the Odyssey we read
that young people are always lacking in wisdom (vii, 294), and
characteristically Telemachos, when offered advice by the goddess
Athene in the guise of Mentes, says that she has advised him with
friendly heart 'as a father does his son' (i, 307–8). Nestor combines the
authority of both parent and ancient, while Phoenix, in addressing
Achilles, fulfils the duty of a father towards his young charge. But in
the Works and Days the pattern is changed, and, instead of a father
advising his son, a brother corrects his brother and we cannot be
certain that Hesiod is even the elder of the two (pp. 84–5). This is a new
feature and one which is missing from the texts, both Near Eastern and
Greek, which we have been comparing with Hesiod throughout
chapter four. The actual existence of a brother named Perses and of
a quarrel between him and Hesiod supplies a reason for the change in
pattern (p. 105). At the same time one wonders whether there was any
text circulating in the Near East before Hesiod's own times which
incorporated the new theme, whose two essentials would be a pair of
brothers, one good and one bad, and a dispute between them over their
father's property which culminates in a redress to law. If there was
such a story current in the Near East, it is possible that it also contributed
to the change in pattern.

One possibility is the Egyptian myth of Osiris, Seth, and Horus, for
the destruction of Osiris by his younger brother Seth provides one of
our two essentials, while the dispute between Seth and Horus suggests
the other.[34] But much more convincing is a Hurrian myth which we
know from a Hittite version, although some of its details, such as the
home land of Appu and the list of gods and their respective homes,
point clearly to an origin further to the east in Mesopotamia. This
story concerns a man named Appu and his two sons, Bad and Good.[35]
Appu was a person who possessed great wealth but had neither son
nor daughter. This regrettable state of affairs was rectified when Appu

one day, while on his way to offer a lamb to the Sun-god, met the god
in person disguised as a young man. Appu was told to go home to his
wife, and in the meantime the Sun-god interceded on behalf of Appu
with the Storm-god. As a result Appu's wife became pregnant and in
due course gave birth to a son. The proud parent, like Kumarbi in the
Song of Ullikummi (p. 7), fondling the child on his knees, conferred
on his offspring a name; he was given the name of Bad, because the
gods had not at first been favourably disposed to grant Appu's wish
that he should have a child. But now his wife went on to become
pregnant a second time, and to his second son Appu gave the name of
Good. We then lose sight of Appu and pick up the story of the two
brothers when they have attained manhood. The contrast between
their characters corresponded to the difference in their names: thus
we find that brother Bad proposed to Good that they should follow the
example set them by the gods and live their own separate lives apart
from one another; this meant a division of the property which they had
inherited from Appu, and Bad seized the opportunity to swindle his
brother. Luckily the Sun-god was watching what was taking place on
earth when apparently Bad attempted to trick Good by choosing
a good cow for himself but handing over to Good an inferior animal.
At this juncture the Sun-god went into action, but at this juncture
also our text comes to a premature end, although a fragment appears
to describe another episode in the career of the two brothers, who, it
seems, were forced to go to law. Nevertheless, even as we know it at
present, the story of Bad and Good is remarkably like that of Hesiod
and Perses: in both cases we are dealing with a pair of brothers, one
praiseworthy and the other a rogue, who quarrel over a division of
their father's property, and their dispute leads to a legal action. The
Sun-god plays a prominent part in the Hurrian myth, just as Hesiod's
poem makes frequent mention of Zeus. The main difference between
the two texts is that the story of Appu and his two sons has a mythological setting and not the realistic colouring of the Works and Days, since
the Sun-god appears to Appu, and it is in the presence of the Sun-god
that the court case is held.

So far nothing has been said about the Days. Critics remain sharply
divided between those who have little or no hesitation in accepting
this part of the poem as the authentic work of Hesiod and others who
are equally certain that the Days must be excluded from the original
composition. Let me say at the very beginning that I firmly hold to
the opinion that the onus of proof lies with the second group, and that

we ought to accept the Days, unless we have some compelling reason for regarding it as a later addition to the text of the poem. It is ridiculous to attempt to settle the question by relying not on evidence contained within the Days but on preconceived theories about the date of the Greek calendar. The decipherment of Linear B has meant that we can no longer claim Hesiod's Lenaion (verse 504) as our earliest example of a month name in Greek. There will always be many gaps in our knowledge of the ancient world and its institutions, and we must, therefore, abandon the kind of argument which assumes that the Greeks had no calendar before the seventh century B.C., and so it was impossible for Hesiod *c.* 700 B.C. to have composed the Days.

The trouble with the Days is that it does not conform to what modern critics consider to be an adequate conclusion to a poem, but the difficulty is one of our own making, since we are imposing on Greek epic standards which are in no way applicable. I said earlier in this chapter (p. 83) that the Days lies outside the limits of the main compositional ring represented by the *prooemium* and the description of the two Erides on the one hand, and Hesiod's remarks about Pheme and its dangers on the other. It does not automatically follow, however, that Hesiod did not compose the Days. Do the verses which terminate the Days provide only the Days with a conclusion, or do they form the end of the whole Works and Days? I should think that the first possibility is the more likely of the two, but this again, I would stress, does not compel us to dismiss the Days from our list of the works of Hesiod. I should like to be able to accept the suggestion that in the Works and Days we have a progression starting with ages in the myth of the ages, continued by the year in the farmer's calendar, and finishing with the individual days of the month, but I cannot convince myself that such a scheme underlies the structure of Hesiod's poem. I prefer myself to argue that the Days is a natural sequel to the end of the Works: the final section of the Works presents us with a list of things which we should not do, some of them being a matter of commonsense (verses 707 ff.), while others are the result of religious tabu (verses 724 ff.); the Days extends the same list but differs inasmuch as it tells us the particular day when something or other should not be done and also recommends, as well as prohibits, certain actions.

If it can be demonstrated that the Days has been influenced by the Near East, this will help us to ascribe it to Hesiod, for then we may argue that both parts of the Works and Days belong together in the same East Mediterranean tradition. If Herodotus is to be trusted,

Greek poets – and here Herodotus must have had Hesiod in mind – used Egyptian information in associating gods with particular months and days, and also relied on Egyptian sources for horoscope material (2, 82, 1). Calendars of lucky and unlucky days are found among the Egyptians, and, by a curious coincidence, a good example occurs on the back of our papyrus text of the Instruction of Amen-em-Opet (pp. 86–7). This calendar covers the whole year with the exception of the five epagomenal days, and each day of the year is divided into three equal parts. Every part is marked either good or bad, so that some days are completely favourable, some completely bad, and others part good and part evil (cf. Works and Days, 810 and 820–1).[36] Hemerologies, however, are common in Mesopotamia, and there are a number of reasons why we ought to look to that region for the background of Hesiod's Days, especially the fact that Hesiod's month is a lunar month. Babylonian influence has also been detected in the fact that the seventh of the month is said by Hesiod to be the birthday of Apollo (verse 771), since this appears to suggest the use of the hebdomadal system.[37] We have already discussed the possibility that its association with the Babylonian god Shamash may explain why Hesiod says what he does say about the child born on the twentieth of the month (pp. 92–3).

It is generally considered that Hesiod had a choice of three methods at his disposal when it came to adding up the days of the month. First, he could add them up in order, commencing at one and ending with the thirtieth; secondly, he might divide the month into two halves corresponding to the waxing and waning of the moon (verses 772–3, 780, and 798); finally, it was possible for him to split the month into three decades (e.g. verses 819–20). But it has been argued that it is mistaken to suppose that Hesiod could count the days continuously throughout the month.[38] The three days which have been taken to imply a method of continuous counting all fall into a special class: the twentieth and thirtieth are fixed points in the decadic system, while the twenty-seventh has a special name obtained by multiplying the magic numbers three and nine, and a name, moreover, which, according to Hesiod (verse 818), few employ. This argument leaves Hesiod with the second and third methods of dividing the month, that is, either into two halves or three decades. It means that the day referred to in verse 820 must be the twenty-fourth and not, as has been suggested, the twenty-first.[39] In the case of both methods we may assume that the poet counted from one onwards: the fourth of the waning month (verse 798) then becomes the eighteenth, as the fourteenth, a very holy day (verses 819–20), rather than the evil fifteenth (verses 802–4), would rate as the day of the full moon; the eighteenth thus fills the only gap in the days between the fourth and the twentieth.

The list of the days of the month in the sequence adopted by Hesiod comprises the thirtieth, first, fourth, seventh, eighth, ninth, eleventh, twelfth, thirteenth, sixteenth, sixth, eighth, twelfth, twentieth, tenth, fourteenth, eighteenth, fourth, the three fifths, seventeenth, fourth, nineteenth, ninth, twenty-seventh, fourth, fourteenth, and twenty-fourth: the days ignored are the second, third, twenty-first, twenty-second, twenty-third, twenty-sixth, twenty-eighth, and twenty-ninth. A first impression suggests that the order of days is utterly chaotic, but on a closer inspection a pattern begins to emerge, and it is seen that the Days falls into three parts. After the initial mention of the thirtieth day we follow the days from the first to the sixteenth (verse 782). In fact the break comes after the thirteenth, for with the sixteenth we have the decadic method of counting preferred for the first time. A break after the thirteenth is necessary, if Hesiod did not count the full thirty days of the month in numerical order but either used decades or cut the month into two halves, the first of which stopped at the fourteenth. From now on we abandon a strictly numerical treatment of the month, and in the next section of the Days it is subject-matter which offers a link as we learn when, and when not, to have a son or daughter. In this connection it should be noted that the two days which Hesiod associates with a god are the days of their birth, the seventh for Apollo (verse 771) and the fifth for Horkos (verses 803–4). The middle sixth is all right for the birth of a boy but not a girl (verses 782 ff.); the same is true of the first sixth, which is also the right time to castrate kids and sheep; you should choose the eighth for gelding the boar and bull, and the twelfth for mules; the twentieth sees the birth of the clever boy, while the tenth is suitable for a boy and the middle fourth for a girl. Then we meet our second break, for the fourths of the month appear to have had a special significance for Hesiod, who goes on to consider the days in groups. The pattern of this final part of the Days is set when Hesiod refers to the fourth days of the waning and waxing month (verses 797–9). Before he closes the Days by mentioning in turn the fourth, middle fourth, and the fourth after the twentieth (verses 819–21), Hesiod has included all the fifths, the middle seventh, the middle and first ninths and the thrice ninth, interrupting the sequence only to reintroduce the fourth in verse 809. The Days, therefore, forms a carefully arranged list which can reasonably be attributed to Hesiod himself.

We have now completed our study of the Works and Days. We began by examining the instruction type of text and saw how it can be given a narrative setting. Trouble in the law courts is a commonplace idea in the literature of the Near East, and much of Hesiod's advice to Perses had been stated long before the poet's own lifetime. We have discussed the Sumerian farmers' almanac and its programme of a year's work on the farm. The story of two brothers who quarrel over possessions forms part of the plot of the Hurrian myth of Appu. Yet, in spite of the analogies which I have attempted to establish, there remains one great difference when the Near Eastern background of the Works and Days is assessed and the results are compared to those already obtained for the Theogony. There is no one Near Eastern text which parallels the contents of the Works and Days as Enuma Elish does those of the Theogony. We saw at the end of chapter two that the Babylonian creation epic has a special value as a work which appears to date from the period after the collapse of the Mycenaean civilization. It could have become known to the Greeks only when contact with the outside world was re-established around 800 B.C. If influence from the Near East can be shown to be as late as roughly a century or less before Hesiod's own times, then the circumstances of the poet's life and conditions in contemporary Boeotia are of the greatest importance and must be investigated. Our evidence for Boeotia in the eighth and seventh centuries B.C. is mainly archaeological and suffers from the limitations of archaeological evidence. Fortunately, it may be supplemented by what Hesiod himself has to say, especially in the autobiographical passages from the Works and Days; in the next chapter, as in this one, therefore, we shall be more concerned with the Works and Days than with the Theogony. In addition to Hesiod and Perses, we shall find ourselves discussing a third party, their father. Some might think it difficult to be enthusiastic about a person whose very name is unknown, but I have always had a warm regard for the father of Hesiod and Perses. His unenviable career, marked by failure both as a trader and as a parent, will command the sympathy of all except the most hard-hearted reader. Perhaps our opinion of his ability will need to be modified as we consider what Hesiod has to tell us about him.

Chapter V

HESIOD AND BOEOTIA

IN the first four chapters of the book we have surveyed texts from the Near East which parallel the contents of either the Theogony or the Works and Days. We have done this in the hope of being better able to assess the influence of Near Eastern ideas and literature on the two poems by Hesiod. But once it is accepted that the poems reflect influence coming from outside the Greek world, a second question poses itself. By what routes and exactly when was such an influence transmitted? If the argument set forth in the preceding chapters is justified, it should be possible to answer, or at least to outline an answer to, the second question. The Theogony has already yielded valuable clues, for I have attempted to show that, while it is foolish to discount the Mycenaean era as a period of time when ideas were freely exchanged throughout the East Mediterranean, Marduk, the hero of Enuma Elish, is the god most like Zeus in the Theogony, and that the date of the Babylonian Epic of Creation indicates that influence continued to spread westward in the centuries following the Dorian Invasion of Greece. Something, however, more definite than this is needed if we are to get to grips with the problem of transmission. Of course, Hesiod's own date imposes a firm chronological limit on the scope of our investigation, and this is why, in my final chapter, I intend to discuss the evidence for the life of Hesiod and conditions in Boeotia at the time when the poet lived. But I shall be concerned neither exclusively nor even primarily with recovering a date for Hesiod; even if we confined our attention to the question of Hesiod's date, it would be necessary to consider a mass of related, but less specific, evidence. By not restricting myself so narrowly, I hope that the end of chapter five will see us better equipped to understand not only when but also by what route influence was transmitted from the Near East to Greece.

The place to commence any discussion of Hesiod's life is the autobiographical passages from the Works and Days. First we must define our attitude towards these passages, for critics have not always accepted them at their face value. Thus – although it should be noted that this was over sixty years ago – Gilbert Murray refused to believe Hesiod's account of the quarrel with his brother Perses.[1] Such an attitude soon leaves us with no Perses, no father, and even, though here Murray did not commit himself, no poet named Hesiod. If an extreme position has its attractions, it can be argued that the story of the two brothers bitterly opposed to one another is merely a very convenient literary device, possessing no foundation in fact: the situation described by Hesiod is pure invention, designed to provide an appropriate setting for his moral and practical advice; the whole story is a set piece and nothing more. It then becomes absurd for us to expect to extract any reliable evidence from Hesiod's remarks about himself and his family. According to this argument, Hesiod is as slight an historical figure as Homer, and a Homer, moreover, of the type popular in the nineteenth century, the rather clumsy patchworker whose original contribution to the Iliad and the Odyssey was strictly limited. This approach to the autobiographical passages, however, immediately involves one in difficulties and contradictions. If we are loath to accept the quarrel or to consider Hesiod a man of flesh and blood, we then have to explain why, in the second half of the Works and Days, we read those details about his father's journey across the Aegean from Aeolis to Boeotia, for surely they are irrelevant to the main purpose of the poem. It may be argued, I suppose, although I find the argument far-fetched, that this reference does form an integral part of Hesiod's advice on trading at sea, since it stresses the uncertainties of the occupation more effectively by using an illustration drawn from actual life. An easier way to avoid the dilemma, however, is to regard the passage as an interpolation. But other problems remain. If Perses existed only in Hesiod's imagination, why did the poet not prefer a mythological setting for his words of wisdom, as Phoenix does in the Iliad when he tries to win over his young ward Achilles, or as Hesiod himself appears to have done in his Maxims of Chiron? Even more to the point is the question why Hesiod abandons the standard pattern of a father instructing his son, and selects a brother as the person needing instruction. This modification in the pattern would seem to be explicable only if we allow the actual existence of brother Perses and the outbreak of a real and serious quarrel between the brothers over the division of their inheritance. To that extent, the existence of Perses and the occurrence of a quarrel, we must be faced with a true experience of life in the Works and Days.

Yet if these arguments carry weight and the possibility of a legal process between Hesiod and Perses is admitted, we can still minimize its importance and claim that it played the same part for Hesiod as, for example, their love affairs did for the Roman poets.[2] The difficulty here seems to me to have been caused by our inability to reconstruct the course of the quarrel and to describe what happened in neat legal terms. We do not know as yet, and probably never shall know, whether the pair of brothers quarrelled once or twice, or if their dispute ever reached a court of law. Hesiod does not tell us enough; he simply does not bother to fill in the details for us. Nevertheless, this must not be taken to imply that he was not really interested in the quarrel except inasmuch as it offered a situation which he could exploit for a literary purpose. I would agree that it is sheer nonsense to suppose that the Works and Days was composed solely with an impending trial in view; it is certainly much more than a piece of propaganda with which Hesiod hoped to gain the support of the local judges. At the same time, it is possible to trace the influence of the quarrel and to identify a preoccupation with the law throughout both the Theogony and the Works and Days.[3] We must, therefore, recognize that the dispute with Perses was a decisive event in the life of Hesiod and an event which was to play a crucial part in shaping the pattern of his thought. It is true that Hesiod takes full advantage of the quarrel and attaches to it instructions having a universal, and not only a particular, relevance, but the quarrel is still something which coloured his whole outlook on life and something from which he was never able to escape. In both his poems Hesiod lets us see the way in which his mind worked to no lesser extent than Archilochus does. The Works and Days is an intensely personal poem. Acknowledge this and you will be compelled to admit the truth of what Hesiod has to say about himself, his brother, and his father. Acknowledge this and you will be compelled to cease regarding the autobiographical passages as if they supplied odd scraps of information of no great significance in themselves. The personal quarrels of Hesiod and of Archilochus interested the poets themselves, interested their community, and, what is more surprising, interested many others, for even in their own lifetime many of those in their audience cannot have been fellow-citizens.

The most revealing of the autobiographical passages is the one in which we learn about the poet's father. 'When the right time for sailing comes along, drag your boat down to the sea and get a suitable cargo aboard if you want to bring some profit into the house. This is how that father, yours and mine, Perses, used to sail on ships in pursuit of his livelihood. He once came here after a long voyage from Cyme in Aeolis, forced not by wealth but by poverty. He found himself a home near Helicon at Ascra, an awful village, wretched in winter, impossible in summer, and never much good' (verses 630–40). In this extract Hesiod tells us four facts about his father: he had made his living as a sea-trader; he came to Boeotia from Cyme in Aeolis; it was poverty which caused him to leave Asia Minor; and he settled at Ascra near Mount Helicon. This precious information has not been without its critics. Let me refer to two scholars on the passage, the first an ancient and the other a modern historian, so that we may see the kind of difficulty which we should be prepared to face. We know that Ephorus was troubled by the reason which Hesiod gives for his father settling in Greece. He suggested that it was not trade that brought him across the Aegean but that he was in fact a fugitive from a charge of murder; flight is the normal practice for an assassin in the Homeric poems, and it is clear that Ephorus had in mind a famous literary precedent, Odysseus' impersonation of a fleeing homicide.[4] But what is interesting is the fact that Ephorus had to find a more satisfactory reason than that given by Hesiod to account for the father's departure from Asia Minor; the idea that Boeotia might have offered the chance of a better life appears to have struck Ephorus as being strange and so he fell back on this alternative suggestion.

The reluctance of some scholars to accept what Hesiod says is best exemplified by a footnote in Beloch's history of Greece.[5] Like Ephorus, Beloch found the idea that anybody should return to mainland Greece a mystery: the whole story, he maintains, of a sea-trader from Cyme, having met with no success there, becoming a farmer in the interior of Boeotia is utterly ridiculous. Hesiod himself makes it perfectly clear what a struggle the farmer had to undertake in order to scratch a living from the soil, and we all know of the great hunger for land which led to the spread of Greek colonization. Yet here we have a man who returned to Greece! Where did he find land to settle? At the beginning of the twentieth century a person who sought a better life left Europe and went off to the New World; in preferring what to the Greeks counted as the Old World, Hesiod's father seems to have taken the wrong direction. Whatever one thinks of the contemporary analogy, both Beloch and, long before Beloch, Ephorus appreciated that in this piece of biography we appear to have something which conflicts with our picture of conditions in the mainland of Greece. The poet's father returned to Greece at a time when we should expect emigrants to have been flocking out of the motherland. We can understand Archilochus quitting Paros and setting out for Thasos because of poverty, but not Hesiod's father preferring Boeotia to Aeolis.[6] The answer to the problem proposed by Ephorus has the merits of being on the right lines. Rather than dismiss the story and call it ridiculous, as Beloch does, we must try to explain the apparent anomaly.

Why, then, did the father of Hesiod decide to return to Boeotia and ignore the promise held out by the foundation of colonies overseas? There is one simple answer: perhaps when he left Asia Minor the first of these new settlements had yet to be established and he had, therefore, no option but to go back to Greece itself. This may well seem a big assumption, but there is evidence to suggest that the answer is the right one. Tradition claimed Cyme in Italy as the first Greek colony in the West.[7] We know that the colony was founded by the Chalcidians and the Eretrians of Euboea; men from Cyme also joined the party, and there appears to be no reason why we ought to make this contingent come from Cyme in Euboea rather than from Aeolic Cyme, especially when we are told that they were citizens of the state in Asia Minor. But how did men living on the other side of the Aegean come to associate themselves with colonists from Euboea? Hesiod's remarks about his father provide the missing link. This man was only one of a number who left Cyme and came back to Greece about the same time. At this date colonization in the West had not commenced. For many of the Cymaeans, however, conditions in Boeotia proved to be as difficult as they had been before at home, and so quite a few of them were ready to join with the Euboeans when, a few years later, they began to plant their first colonies in the Central Mediterranean. Hesiod's father, who had succeeded in making a new life for himself and was moderately prosperous, was content to stay put when his companions of a few years back made up their minds to try again, this time in Italy, where there was land for the asking.[8] Even if the suggestion that it was Cymaean emigrants to Boeotia who set out to colonize Italy is disallowed, the foundation of the new Cyme must reflect the kind of growing economic pressure and poverty which Hesiod quotes as the reason for his father's emigration. In this way also we may argue for a connection between the foundation of Cyme in Italy and the father's arrival in Boeotia.

The reconstruction of events suggested above is of the greatest importance, since it offers a clue as to the date of Hesiod. If the date when Cyme in Italy was founded can be fixed, we have only to go back a few years before that date in order to determine when the Cymaean contingent left their homes in Aeolic Cyme. Presumably they were not in Boeotia very long before they were persuaded to pack their bags again and try their luck somewhere else; Hesiod's parent would have come to Greece with them, and thus we can arrive at the approximate date of his voyage across the Aegean. Hesiod's poetry may then be placed a generation, say thirty years, later. If the Thucydidean chronology for the Sicilian colonies is accepted, and we allow some twenty years between the settlements at Cyme and Syracuse, the foundation of Cyme must be dated to *c.* 750 B.C. or slightly before; this in turn suggests approximately 760 as the date when Hesiod's father reached Greece and a *floruit* about 730 for Hesiod himself. That the Theogony was composed after 750 B.C. is implied by Hesiod's reference to Delphi (verses 497–500), which falls into the same category as the references to that place in the Iliad (ix, 404–5) and the Odyssey (viii, 79–81).[9] However, since Dunbabin wrote on the Western Greeks, the dangers of an uncritical acceptance of the Thucydidean chronology have been underlined by new evidence, which makes it advisable that we date the foundation of Cyme between 750 and 725 rather than at 750 B.C.[10] If we adopt a similar elasticity in the case of the other two dates, we are left with our poet dangling between 730 and 705 B.C. Although so vague a date seems to be of limited value, it does serve to counteract a recent tendency to place the Theogony well into the seventh century. Thus Kirk, on the basis of a linguistic comparison with the Iliad and the Homeric Hymns, dates the composition of the Theogony not earlier than around 675, while the poem, according to Starr, who doubts that its author was the Hesiod who composed the Works and Days, is a product of the early or mid-seventh century.[11] In spite of the present uncertainty as to the date of the Sicilian colonies, I still feel that 730 B.C. is the correct date for Hesiod, and I am reluctant to abandon a Cyme first established halfway through the eighth century. Yet I realize that my reluctance is prompted by personal views about Hesiod and his poetry.

The date of Cyme, in my opinion, is the only firm evidence that we have for the date of Hesiod, and here, as we have seen, our conclusions must be qualified and we must admit that we cannot do better than suggest the general period between 730 and 705 B.C. Although it is not possible to be more positive, this evidence is important inasmuch as it shows that Hesiod lived in the eighth and not the seventh century B.C. To date the Theogony as late as 650 and to refuse it to Hesiod is a theory to be rejected. But even if we have no other firm evidence for the date of Hesiod, we may ask whether there is any additional evidence which will at least suggest that Starr's date for the Theogony is impossibly

late. In this respect we may consider what one type of archaeological
evidence has to offer us. Can we identify any picture dating from the
first half of the seventh century B.C. which appears to be an illustration
of Hesiod and therefore to imply a knowledge of his poetry? The
Theogony with its wealth of mythological references might well have
stimulated the imagination of artists within a few years of its composition. This is a fresh approach to the problem of dating the poem,
although such evidence has been employed in an attempt to establish
the date of the Aspis. But I should add that the conclusions reached by
the two scholars to have considered the evidence do not agree.[12] Those
discussing Homer have often examined the identification of scenes on
vases. The evidence is notoriously difficult to interpret and the limitations of such material are well known.[13] If we do find a likely picture,
we have first to make up our minds whether it is a mythological picture
or an illustration of everyday life. If we then decide in favour of the
former alternative, we must still identify the particular myth illustrated.
A classic example is offered by the Rape of Helen vase from the British
Museum. Is this just a picture of a man bidding farewell to his wife or
an abduction scene? Are we faced with an actual or a mythological
incident? If the latter, what myth forms the subject of the picture?
It is not surprising that so many couples other than Paris and Helen
have been thought to be depicted on this vase. Nevertheless, in spite of
all these complications, every now and again an exciting new identification is suggested, and once more we eagerly review the evidence. Thus,
now over ten years ago, Roland Hampe published a geometric jug
decorated on the neck with a possible picture of Odysseus sitting on the
keel of his upturned boat (cf. Odyssey xii, 420–5).[14] Lately it has been
suggested that another geometric jug illustrates the end of the duel
fought between Ajax and Hector in the seventh book of the Iliad
(verses 206 ff.).[15] Such identifications inspire the hope that one day we
shall isolate an eighth-century illustration which can be referred to
a passage in the Homeric poems so convincingly that it will be acceptable to all. But even a certain identification will not necessarily establish
a knowledge of the poems by Homer, for it can always be referred to
earlier material incorporated in the Iliad or the Odyssey. This final
complication will concern us when we reach our second illustration of
the Theogony.

I now want to consider two possible illustrations of the Theogony.
I do not propose to say anything about early pictures of Heracles or the
kind of picture in which a god or hero is matched against a dragon, as

the subject-matter here is too general for it to be related directly to anything said by Hesiod.[16] I would stress that the very fact that I do have examples to discuss suggests what the future may hold in store for us. The excavations at Perachora led to the discovery of a relief plaque of terra-cotta, decorated with the figure of a standing woman. A line of black dots running around the chin is thought to represent a beard. The lower part of the figure is concealed in what is described as a sack or bag with two protuberances at the bottom. The treatment of the woman's body and dress, the picture of Pegasos on the back, and the type of clay used show that the plaque is of Corinthian manufacture, but the round head of the woman suggests oriental influence. Such details lead to the suggestion that on this plaque 'the scene portrayed is a Grecized version of the bisexual Aphrodite of the Orient and Cyprus being born from the severed genitals of Ouranos'.[17] The object is assigned to the first half of the seventh century B.C. with the second quarter of that century preferred. Is the picture on this plaque, made apparently in Corinth, based on the description of the birth of the goddess in the Theogony (verses 180 ff.) or is it inspired by some other source? If it is inspired by Hesiod's poem, it will serve to confirm my argument that it is wrong to date the Theogony much after 700 B.C.

That the woman depicted on the plaque is Aphrodite being born from someone's genitals appears to be beyond question. It is true that we have no proof that these are the organs of Ouranos, but it is a tall order to expect the craftsman responsible for the work to have indicated whose genitals they are supposed to be. I am not troubled because this Aphrodite appears to have a beard. All that Hesiod says about the physical appearance of his goddess is that she was beautiful (verse 194). This is merely a conventional epithet, and, while we may hesitate a little at the thought of a bearded lady being called beautiful, I am at a loss to see how it can be claimed that 'it seems quite out of the question that the artisan who made this figurine drew upon the text of the Theogony, because the Hesiodic Aphrodite is very far from being bearded'.[18] Hesiod tells us nothing about Aphrodite's looks. The Theogony and the plaque may be independent of one another but reflect the same traditional story of the birth of Aphrodite from male sexual organs. It is, however, equally possible that the maker of the plaque had the passage from the Theogony in mind, and that here we have a conscious illustration of Hesiod. The Theogony would then have been composed before the manufacture of the plaque, whenever that may have been within the first half of the seventh century B.C.

My other illustration also relates to a passage in the Theogony. It will be found on the magnificent Protoattic amphora recovered during the summer of 1954 in the cemetery at Eleusis.[19] The main panel of the vase – and this is the largest decorative panel known to us – depicts the myth of Perseus, who is shown fleeing from the two surviving Gorgons after he had beheaded their sister Medusa. On one side lies the headless body of Medusa, stretched on its back in the middle of a flowery meadow. Next come the two Gorgons in pursuit, then Athene who checks their advance, and finally we have Perseus and a large bird; little of the figure of Perseus survives apart from his legs. The neck of the amphora on the main side is also decorated with a mythological picture, which shows the blinding of Polyphemus by Odysseus. In his description of the vase Mylonas claims that its painter in the blinding scene follows the Homeric account of the incident, but eliminates details such as the setting in the cave and reduces the number of Odysseus' companions from four to two. The modifications are dictated by the restricted area available for decoration. The face of Polyphemus is shown in profile, and the Cyclops has an eye placed in the normal position on the human face. Mylonas points out that, whereas Homer credits Polyphemus with only one eye, he does not specify where that eye was located. The first reference to its being positioned in the middle of the forehead of the Cyclopes is provided by the Theogony (verses 143–5). Mylonas, therefore, concludes, although the conclusion seems to me to be a very rash one, that the painter did not know the reference to the monsters in the Theogony, for otherwise, Mylonas claims, he would have sited the eye in the middle of Polyphemus' forehead. Mylonas is far too extravagant in his estimate of the artist's ability in this as in other respects; surely it is folly to assume that so early a painter of such a scene could have mastered what remained a constant problem, namely how to represent a monster with an eye placed in the centre of his forehead.[20] I have dealt with the picture of Polyphemus and the position of his eye at some length, because Mylonas, having thus assumed that its painter did not follow the Theogony, is obliged to argue that the main picture similarly owes nothing to Hesiod. Yet there is one detail which suggests that the reverse is true.

Hesiod refers to three Gorgons, one of them, Medusa, liable to death, and the other two, Sthenno and Euryale, immortal (verses 274 ff.). Poseidon is said to have lain beside Medusa in a soft meadow, amid spring flowers, a detail which fits in nicely with the background of the picture on Mylonas' vase. Perseus cut off her head and consequently Chrysaor and Pegasos were born. Hesiod makes no mention of Athene nor does he comment on the flight of Perseus. The vase does not feature the birth of Chrysaor and Pegasos, while the bird with fully opened wings, perhaps an eagle, is another problem. Nevertheless, in spite of these inconsistencies between the Theogony and the picture, I would suggest that the latter illustrates the former. We must certainly allow the painter as much latitude in this picture as Mylonas is prepared to allow him in his rendering of the Polyphemus scene. Here Mylonas takes into account both Homer's vagueness and the small area on the neck of the amphora available for decoration. The same concessions, that is, for the space factor and for the brevity of Hesiod's description of Perseus, should be made for the other picture. To have included the offspring of Medusa in addition to two Gorgons, Athene, Perseus, and the bird would not have been easy, and I fail to see how the artist could have found sufficient room for Chrysaor and Pegasos on either side of the outstretched body of Medusa. But I have yet to mention a striking recollection of the Theogony: the two surviving Gorgons are not identical, and their different appearance, one being stronger and the other more agile, corresponds exactly to the difference between Hesiod's pair of Gorgons as it is implied by the meaning of their names, Sthenno and Euryale.[21] We have, therefore, to assume either a source in popular tradition common to both Hesiod and the painter, or – and this, unlike Mylonas, I think likely to be the right answer – that the Polyphemus painter is influenced by the Theogony. The date of the vase is important: Mylonas places it in the second quarter of the seventh century B.C. and, moreover, towards the beginning of that period, since he regards it as our earliest example of the Black and White style.[22]

It is the relief pithos, however, that one particularly associates with early illustrations of Greek mythology and Boeotia. A superb example of the type, decorated with reliefs portraying the Fall of Troy, was found in 1961 on the island of Mykonos.[23] More important for Hesiod is another relief pithos, this time from the island of Tenos, the neck of which is decorated with a picture of a winged goddess, who sits with outstretched arms on a throne; from her head there springs another winged figure, armed with a helmet, a spear, and perhaps a thunderbolt.[24] If, as seems the only possible interpretation of the relief, this picture shows the birth of one deity from the head of another, the armed figure must be Athene, but the seated figure is clearly a female

and cannot, therefore, be Zeus. It is, presumably, Metis, and the artist
follows a tradition which made Metis not only pregnant with Athene
but also the actual person who gave birth to the goddess.[25] This is not
the story told by Hesiod in the Theogony (verses 886 ff.), but,
remembering the Boeotian background of the relief pithoi and the date
of the Tenos vase (*c.* 700 B.C.), I would suggest that there may be
a connection between vase and Theogony in the prominence of Metis
according to both versions of the myth. What is fascinating, but
incapable of proof, is the possibility that the vase represents the basic
form of the myth which Hesiod has modified, so that it conforms to the
story of Ouranos and the offspring of Ouranos and that of Kronos and
his children. Also suggestive is Enuma Elish and its story of how Ea
acquired the wisdom of Mummu at the time when Apsu's plot against
the gods was foiled (p. 34).

Although the fact that they share a stock of common formulas and
themes makes it absurd to argue that Homer and Hesiod provide
evidence of imitation, the situation changes when orally composed
poetry gives way to written literature. Provided that a poet who relies
on writing to compose his verses is early enough in date, it is relevant
that we should ask whether this poet appears to know his Hesiod. The
question must be asked of Archilochus, whose *floruit* appears to coincide
with the middle of the seventh century B.C.[26] If it can be suggested that
Archilochus was acquainted with the work of Hesiod, we shall have
another reason for believing that our date of Hesiod in the late eighth
century is correct, for, obviously, a little time must be allowed for the
spread of Hesiod's reputation. If Hesiod, moreover, is shown to have
influenced Archilochus, this will strengthen my argument that he also
influenced Greek artists living at the same period of time. But absolute
proof once again is not possible, and we have to wait until Alcaeus at
the end of the seventh century before meeting a passage of which we
may say with complete confidence that its author set out to reproduce
a piece of Hesiod.[27]

We know something today of Archilochus' story of his own inaugura-
tion as a poet. It appears to have included the loss of a cow, the
acquisition of a lyre, and some mysterious women, who, like the cow,
vanish into thin air. It can hardly be imagined that the poet meant his
audience to take this story for a sober piece of autobiography and it has
been aptly called 'a mocking reminder of Hesiod's serious claim'.[28]
Archilochus' claim to be the servant of lord Enyalios and to know the
lovely gift of the Muses calls to mind Hesiod's description of the

rhapsode as the servant of the Muses (cf. fr. 8 and Theogony, 99–100 and 103). Another fragment which tells of the ability of the gods to raise up the downtrodden and to trip up the successful (fr. 123) preaches from the same text as the opening lines of the Works and Days. Such a sentiment, however, is commonplace. More revealing is the use by Archilochus of the animal fable, since here he follows in the steps of Hesiod, the author of the story of the hawk and the nightingale (Works and Days, 202–12). In the prayer which the fox addresses to father Zeus when the eagle has broken its agreement and carried off the foxcubs we hear echoes of the part of the Works and Days which follows Hesiod's fable (cf. fr. 171, 1–4, and Works and Days, 213–85, especially 238–9, 267–9, and 276–81). Archilochus narrates the encounter between the fox and the eagle in his first epode, the poem in which he delivered his savage attack on Lykambes. Lasserre believes that this poem was composed when Archilochus was twenty-five or twenty-six, which, by his reckoning, would put it about 685 B.C.[29] This date depends upon our knowing the year of the poet's birth, as well as the year of his life when the first epode was written, so that I quote it more out of interest than out of conviction.

But let us leave the problem of Hesiod's date and see what other information there may be relating to the passage about his father's emigration. So far we have tried to find out why the father should have chosen to return to Boeotia; I want now to ask why he preferred Ascra with its appalling climate to other places in this region of Greece. Hesiod himself seems to give the answer when he says that his father settled in a wretched village Ascra near Helicon, for it is the fact that Ascra lay near Mount Helicon which solves the problem. Ascra, according to Pausanias (9, 29, 1–2), was reputed to have been founded by Ephialtes and Otos, the sons of Aloeus. To substantiate his statement, Pausanias quotes four verses from a poem by Hegesinus, a reference which he himself borrowed from a history of Orchomenos by the Corinthian Callippus. These lines tell how the nymph Ascra lay with the god Poseidon and bore him a son called Oioklos. It was this child, together with the sons of Aloeus, who first founded Ascra at the foot of Mount Helicon. Pausanias also says that it was claimed that Ephialtes and Otos were the first to sacrifice to the Muses on Helicon and consecrate the mountain to the goddesses. From the very beginning, then, a close link joined Ascra and the cult centre of the Muses on Helicon, for the same pair were thought to have established both town and cult. A little later Pausanias talks about people living around the grove of the Muses and claims that the Thespians held a festival there called the Mousaia (9, 31, 3).[30] Hesiod combined the two professions of farmer and singer; his father, while in residence at Ascra, might have likewise combined two occupations, those of farmer and dealer, for a popular place of worship and the occurrence at regular intervals of a well organized festival would have brought the surrounding peoples flocking into Ascra and thus given Hesiod's father an opportunity of displaying his talents as a trader.[31] This may explain why Ascra, in spite of its miserable climate, had a special attraction for an immigrant who had before been a sea-trader. According to Pausanias, the sons of Aloeus believed that there were three Muses, named Melete, Mneme, and Aoide, all three of which names suggest the technique of epic composition. It was while pasturing sheep on the slopes of Helicon that Hesiod was visited by the Muses; the Heliconian Muses were Hesiod's patron goddesses, and it was to them, as we shall shortly see, that he dedicated the tripod which he won at the funeral games of Amphidamas. Son and father, I suggest, were kept in Ascra by more than its agricultural potential, and it is possible that Hesiod maintained a family association with the Heliconian Muses which his father had begun.

Having discussed Ascra, the place where the poet's father ended his travels, I must proceed now to Cyme, the starting-point of his journey across the Aegean Sea. Is it possible that this city in Aeolis supplied a link in the chain of transmission from the Near East to mainland Greece? This, in my opinion, is most unlikely. Too often in the past, whether it is a matter of Aeolic elements in Hesiod's language or oriental influence, we have been reminded that the poet's family came to Greece from Cyme. But in the Works and Days Hesiod merely says that his father came to Boeotia over a vast expanse of sea, having left Cyme in Aeolis (verses 635–6). He does not state that his family had gone to Cyme with the original settlers of the city or even at an early stage in its history; he does not state that his father, when he left, pulled up roots which went very deep. We know that it was from Cyme that he came to Boeotia, and nothing more. We have Hesiod's own words to prove that the poet's experience of travel by sea was restricted to the short crossing from Aulis to the island of Euboea (verses 650–1). It will be vain to search for a reference in the Works and Days which implies a detailed knowledge of places or conditions on the other side of the Aegean.

Yet, as our knowledge of the Phrygians and their capital at Gordion continues to be enriched by excavation in years to come, it is likely that more will be made of the significance of Cyme. Today already it is possible to discuss at some length the trade between the Greeks of Ionia and the Phrygians and the use during the period 730 to 675 B.C. of the overland route across the plateau of Anatolia.[32] This line of communication, however, leads to Urartu and Iran, passing to the north of Mesopotamia which finds its obvious outlet to the West in the ports of North Syria. Apart from the new archaeological evidence, there is one scrap of literary evidence to be considered: Midas, king of Phrygia, is reputed to have married the daughter of Agamemnon of Cyme.[33] Starting from so bare a statement, one scholar has recently built up an impressive picture of Cyme and its relations with the Phrygian monarchy about the last quarter of the eighth century B.C.[34] It is suggested that this Midas is the great Midas, king of Phrygia at the time when Sargon II occupied the Assyrian throne. Strabo's statement (13, 622) that it took the inhabitants of Cyme three hundred years from the date of their city's foundation to appreciate the commercial value of their port is associated with the era of Phrygian thalassocracy; Cyme provided the Phrygians with convenient access to the Aegean. Midas' interest in the oracle at Delphi (Hdt. 1, 14, 2) suggests that the king may have had something to do with the foundation of Cyme in Italy. The name of Agamemnon of Cyme means that he traced his ancestry back to the Greek commander at Troy, and so we have evidence for the survival of Mycenaean traditions among the Aeolic Greeks. The same can also be claimed of contemporary Phrygia provided that the Midas tomb at Yazilikaya is dated in the eighth century and regarded as the tomb of this same great Midas, since the upper inscription on the tomb applies the Mycenaean titles of king and war-leader to Midas. All this leaves one breathless with admiration for Cyme as it might have been in Hesiod's own times, but we have been piling supposition on supposition, ignoring the serious difficulties with which each of these suggestions bristles. Unfortunately, the archaeologist has contributed little as yet to our knowledge of early Cyme.[35] But whatever he may eventually uncover will not alter the fact that Hesiod mentions Cyme only as the place which his father left when he made his way to Boeotia, and I cannot see how this entitles us to assume that in doing this he was severing an association which extended very far back into the past. Actually there is a much better candidate for the route by which the Greeks could have become conversant with Babylonian literature in the eighth century B.C., the route which ran from North Syria to the mainland of Greece. North Syria, as I remarked above, is the natural place for Mesopotamian influence to reach the shores of the Mediterranean. There is definite evidence, moreover, which links the Euboeans with North Syria, and, apart from the influence exerted by the Euboeans on the adjoining parts of Greece, Euboea is the one place that we know Hesiod to have visited. But this brings me to the second autobiographical passage in the Works and Days, and I must say a little about the passage in general before I attempt to develop this particular argument in greater detail.

In the course of his advice on sea-trading, Hesiod interrupts his instructions twice, once to relate what I take to be the most memorable event in his father's life, and then, slightly later, to tell us about his own greatest achievement. This is the story of how he came to win a tripod at the funeral games of Amphidamas of Chalcis (verses 650–9); it was this celebration which persuaded him to take his solitary trip by sea, from Aulis in Boeotia across the narrow channel which separates Boeotia from the island of Euboea. For all its irony, this passage, I imagine, refers to the most arduous journey undertaken by Hesiod, for I do not believe that the poet visited Athens at any stage in his career, nor can Athens be easily accommodated in the scheme of transmission which I wish to advance.[36] It has often been claimed that the reference to Amphidamas in verse 654 provides some indication of Hesiod's date, but I am doubtful of the argument. It depends upon a statement of Plutarch, who says that Amphidamas fell in the Lelantine War (Moralia 153 F). The date of the war, which is itself no small problem, should therefore give us the date of Hesiod. But Hesiod says nothing to throw any light on Plutarch's cryptic notice, and he presents us with no hint of any hostilities between Chalcis and Eretria. 'King' Amphidamas is an elusive character, and any number of objections can be lodged against those who think him reliable evidence of Hesiod's date: several scholars have maintained that there were two separate men with the common family name of Amphidamas, one referred to by Hesiod and the other by Plutarch; at least one has denied Amphidamas any real existence and made Hesiod perform at a ceremony connected with a hero cult.[37] One thing is clear from Hesiod's remarks: the sons of Amphidamas could hardly have been burying the actual body of their father. They proclaimed the games, and the competition must have been keen for Hesiod to have taken so much pride in his

victory; time would have lapsed while Hesiod and the other partici-
pants made their way to Chalcis. The difficulty is neatly evaded by
the claim that Amphidamas was killed in a sea-battle against the
Eretrians. But this can be no hero cult, for Hesiod is describing
a special rather than a regular occasion. Too many are wont to
call Amphidamas king of Chalcis; this is done by neither Hesiod
nor Plutarch, although the scholiast makes Amphidamas king of
Euboea! It is this type of complication which reduces the value of the
reference, but, if it is still felt that its evidence carries weight, it merely
serves to confirm my eighth-century date of Hesiod, as the Lelantine
War probably occurred in the last third of that century.[38]

There is other evidence of a more definite nature to be extracted
from the Amphidamas passage. First, we have a picture of the circumstances which might provide Hesiod with a public. The funeral of
Amphidamas, admittedly, was very much a special event, and Hesiod's
average audience must have been altogether less impressive. Advising
the farmer, he requires the man who wants to succeed to pass by the
warm and insidiously comfortable smithy in winter (verses 493–4).
Habits die hard, especially in a rural community, and to this day your
Greek has a modern equivalent of Hesiod's crowded smithy in the
village coffeehouse; there he meets his friends and the various officials
with whom he has dealings, and there, if Vasilika in present-day
Boeotia is characteristic, he will spend his evenings and, in winter,
much of every day.[39] But there is further evidence to show that funeral
games were being held in Boeotia at a period not far removed from
the time when Hesiod himself lived. This is supplied by archaic
inscriptions coming from the fragmentary remains of nine prizes offered
at funeral games. In the case of such prizes one expects to find two
inscriptions, one inscribed by the donor to celebrate the ceremonies,
and the other added by the person winning the prize, when he dedicated
it at some sanctuary.[40] Parts of five Boeotian prize lebetes (*c.* 700–600?)
have been found at Athens on the Acropolis, a fact which suggests that
these games attracted competitors from over a wide area, so that
Hesiod's long journey to Chalcis is nothing exceptional. Two other
pieces have a special interest for Hesiod – one, a fragment from the
rim of an archaic bronze lebes (*c.* 625–600?), because it was found at
Helicon, and the second, another fragment, actually from Thebes,
because the style of its lettering in the commemoration inscription
suggests a date in the first quarter of the seventh century B.C. The
latter was presented as a prize at the funeral games of a man named

Ekpropos and dedicated to Apollo by a certain Isodikos. The remaining fragments consist of another found at Thebes (*c.* 625–600?) and a sixth-century (*c.* 550?) example from Delphi. Hesiod, therefore, when he mentions his success at Chalcis, seems to be describing an experience which, however special it was for the poet, was by no means unique or even extremely rare in archaic Boeotia.

The funeral games of Amphidamas brought Hesiod to Chalcis in Euboea, and it is Euboea which will take us along the most convincing route to the Near East. What contacts did the Greeks establish with their neighbours in the Near East, once they had recovered from the shocks attending the collapse of the Mycenaean civilization? Every year sees us more able to answer that question. Especially exciting is the proof that Greeks actually settled in some of the ports scattered along the coast of the Levant.[41] We know most about the history of Al Mina, although the dates proposed by its excavator and his reconstruction of events at Al Mina both stand in need of considerable modification as the result of new studies of the Greek and the so-called Cypriot pottery. With Al Mina, furthermore, we have found our way back to the Orontes river, as the port is sited at the mouth of that river. Woolley distinguished ten levels of occupation at Al Mina, perhaps the classical Posideion mentioned by Herodotus (3, 91, 1). They stretched from the middle of the eighth century to the end of the fourth century B.C., when the foundation of Seleucia four miles to the north caused Al Mina to sink into oblivion. Woolley argued that levels X and IX, when much of the pottery was imported from the Greek world, belonged to the period 750–700 B.C. In level VIII the pottery changed to that characteristic of Iron Age Cyprus, and this development was associated with a short-lived Cypriot settlement. The next level, a period again of limited duration, was marked by a decline in the quantity of Cypriot ware and the reappearance of Greek imports. In levels VI and V are found orientalizing style pots coming from Rhodes and Corinth, and then in level IV, after a gap which lasted until about 520 B.C., Athenian imports.[42]

But Woolley's dates are too low, and his views on the place of origin of the pottery types which he lists as found at Al Mina need revision. Of crucial importance for Hesiod is Boardman's study of Euboean pottery, which has suggested that much of the pottery from the earliest strata, previously labelled Cycladic, was produced by the inhabitants of Euboea. He is thus able to argue that the Euboeans played a major, if not the major, part in the establishment of Al Mina; this event he would place towards the beginning of the eighth century, so that it seems that the Euboeans tried exploiting new markets in the East, perhaps in search of metals, before they turned their attention to Italy and Sicily.[43] The Euboeans, in addition, did more than just trade at Al Mina, for there is evidence to suggest that Greek potters took up residence in the port and continued to produce on the site their own pottery.[44]

Syrian and Palestinian pottery appear to carry the establishment of Al Mina back into the ninth century B.C., and it is possible that its foundation took place a short time before the first traders arrived from Greece.[45] It needed Greeks, however, to put Al Mina firmly on the map as an important centre of trade. The history of the site concerns our study of Hesiod only to about 600 B.C. when Babylonian intervention in Syria caused a sharp decline in its fortune. Two periods, one covering levels X to VII and the other levels VI and V, may be distinguished before the sixth century B.C. The break after level VII, when Al Mina may have been abandoned for a brief period, is marked by rebuilding on new lines in level VI and a change in the pattern of trade through the port. In levels VI and V, that is, during the seventh century, East Greek and Corinthian types of pottery replace imports from Euboea. The break is probably to be associated with the activities of the Assyrians, who shortly after the middle of the eighth century under the leadership of Tiglath-pileser III superseded Urartu as the dominant power in the western regions of Asia. The Assyrians were constantly experiencing trouble with their subjects in this part of their empire. Two events are noteworthy, and either may explain the break at Al Mina. After securing his throne, Sargon II had to take the field in 720 B.C. against a hostile coalition of states in Syria and Palestine. In 696 his son and successor, Sennacherib, crushed a rebellion which had broken out in the province of Cilicia; the leader of the rebels appears to have been supported by Greek forces. Either or both of these rebellions may lie behind the collapse of Euboean interests at Al Mina.[46] The year, however, which saw the end of Euboean activities in North Syria is less important for us than the fact that they seem to have been extremely active here during the eighth century, for part of which time the Assyrians were in control of the region. Al Mina is an obvious place for the Greeks to have acquired a knowledge of Enuma Elish or any other work of Babylonian literature composed at a date which makes transmission via the Mycenaeans impossible; a direct line of transmission can then be traced running from Mesopotamia to Al Mina and from North Syria to Euboea. Even if we did not know that Hesiod visited Chalcis in Euboea, it requires a very short step across the Euripus to reach Boeotia.

But it would be wrong to consider only the Euboeans as possible intermediaries between Hesiod and the Near East. It has often been argued that Phoenicians are the missing link in the chain of transmission, and I do not deny their probable importance; one merely regrets that they tend to be so difficult to identify. A new examination of the various types of pottery at Al Mina which Woolley termed Cypriot ware, namely white painted and bichrome, black-on-red, and red slip pottery, has revealed that this had a wider distribution than was previously suspected.[47] The two latter types appear to have spread to Cyprus from Phoenicia and Syria. As a result we can no longer separate Al Mina from the region to the south and we should really talk about a Cypro-Phoenician phase covering our first period at Al Mina. Like its pottery, the population of Al Mina in the eighth century B.C. was a mixture probably of Greeks, Cypriots, and Orientals. It seems likely that the Greeks were a minority group, although they proved more significant than their true numbers might suggest. The role of the Phoenicians is stressed by the recent discovery of Greeks at another port to the south of Al Mina and a port actually on the Phoenician coast. This is Tell Sukas and here, as at Al Mina, the presence of Greek settlers has been noted. At Tell Sukas a destruction *c.* 850 B.C. seems to have been followed by contacts with the Greeks which were maintained until interrupted by another destruction three centuries after the first. These contacts led to Greek settlers establishing themselves at Tell Sukas, and their settlement may go back to the second half of the ninth century B.C., another period when the Assyrians controlled Syria.[48] Tell Sukas represents another mixed community, perhaps as early as that at Al Mina, where the presence of Greeks met with no objection from the local inhabitants. One reference made in the Works and Days should be mentioned at this point. In describing the delights of summer Hesiod advises us to find a shady rock where we can sit, liberally supplied with food and drink. The wine which he specifies is a Bybline vintage (verse 589). It is impossible to be certain what kind of wine Hesiod has in mind, but it may be rather a special variety to match so pleasant an occasion and it could be wine from the Phoenician town of Byblos. If it is, then we have literary evidence with which we may supplement that provided by the archaeologist and a further indication of the trade developing between Greece and the Near East.

It was from the town of Byblos in Phoenicia that the Greeks apparently took their name for a second commodity, papyrus, their usual writing material, presumably because they first met it at that place. A knowledge of material suitable for writing implies a knowledge of the art of writing itself. The latest research suggests that the Phoenician alphabet was introduced into Greece around the middle of the eighth century B.C. or a little later. Extreme caution is necessary when it comes to the selection of the probable place where the Greeks first learnt to write their language in this new script, but Al Mina with its Greek settlers has appealed to some.[49] The tradition that the Greeks learnt their letters from Phoenicians who settled in Boeotia (Hdt. 5, 57–8) ties in well with Al Mina and its Euboeans provided that we substitute for native Phoenicians Greeks who returned home after residence in North Syria. Al Mina, therefore, may be the place where Greeks for the first time not only heard of a poem like Enuma Elish, but also learnt to write. Although no one can say how the individual pieces of the jigsaw fit together, the coincidence of a new type of poetry and the new technique of writing, long used throughout the Near East to record verse, seems too remarkable to be accidental. As was said above, it is a short step from Euboea to Boeotia, and we know that the Euboeans handed their version of the alphabet on to Boeotia, where the earliest datable inscription, a dedication to the god Apollo on a large bronze statuette, the Mantiklos Apollo, reputed to come from Thebes, is surprisingly early and may belong even to the late eighth century B.C. That a knowledge of an exciting new kind of poetry should also have spread to continental Greece need not strain our credulity, especially if writing and poetry marched side by side.

If the island of Euboea, by reason of its intimate contacts with the Near East, played an important part in accelerating the development of Greece, we should expect its immediate neighbour Boeotia to show signs of a relatively progressive culture when compared to that prevalent in other parts of Greece. The influence of the Euboean cities may be seen if we contrast the geographical knowledge of Hesiod and Homer. It is in the West alone that Hesiod can boast any real advantage, and this is not unexpected in the case of a poet linked by a specific reference to one of the states responsible for the colonization of that region.[50] Yet it is not difficult to get the wrong impression from reading the Works and Days. Indeed one scholar spoke of Hesiod as 'a poor peasant farmer, a deadly conservative, embittered against society by a personal pique against his brother, living in a backward section of Greece, off

the main highways of trade, and largely out of touch with the contemporary current of economic and cultural life'.[51] A crushing indict-
ment, but one whose every statement can today be proved ill-founded.
Hampe and others have rescued Boeotia from the prejudices of its
neighbours and drawn a much more convincing picture of Boeotia as
it must have been known to Hesiod. Mythology, art, and poetry all
show that, far from being backward, Boeotia was a centre from which
influence emanated.[52] Without going into detail, I wish to stress the
point, for it reveals the dangers inherent in another method used to date
Hesiod. It is commonly assumed that Hesiod must be later than Homer,
for Hesiod's Works and Days appears to represent a more developed
literary form: the difference between the two poets in technique of
composition and in language is thought to imply a lapse of time. But
Homer and Hesiod come from opposite sides of the Aegean Sea, Ionia
and Boeotia, and yet we argue as if all Greek epic were exposed to the
same type and the same degree of influence and so evolved in the same
way and at the same pace.[53] It is not sufficient to decide the date of
Homer and then tack on Hesiod some twenty or thirty years later;
each poet must be dated independently and only when we have done
that are we entitled to examine the relationship between them.

A more insidious type of argument can result from a comparison of
passages in Homer and Hesiod whose contents or phrasing are similar.
If what we have been taught during the past thirty-five years by the
study of orally composed poetry is ignored, it can be assumed that,
when passages from the two poets exhibit similarities, one of them must
be consciously imitating the other. If it is possible to determine which
passage is the original and which the imitation, then we have also
determined the relative chronology of their authors. Such an approach
has an irresistible appeal if one denies the unity of the Homeric poems,
for, by asking whether their authors influenced Hesiod or were themselves influenced by the Boeotian poet, the different strata which go to
make up our text of Homer may be identified. The Odyssey in particular has provided scholars with much so-called evidence, and the list
of those who have tried to establish the relative date of Homer, or
parts of the Homeric poems, and Hesiod by a comparison of passages
whose contents coincide is long. To compile a list of such scholars
would prove only the futility of their arguments about priority of
composition. Agreement will never be reached, and it is no surprise
that this should be so, for there is no reason why it must be assumed
that similar extracts from the two poets are related in this way to each

other. If poets trained in an oral tradition share formulas and themes, it is inevitable that we meet coincidence of phrasing when their subject-matter is similar. Thus when Hesiod mentions the history of the age of heroes, formulas known to both him and Homer start to flow forth.[54] Lord puts the matter in the right perspective when he compares the knowledge of a large group of formulas by all singers with the knowledge and use of words and phrases by all members of one speech community.[55] If we have a number of passages in Homer and Hesiod whose contents are very alike or even identical, this in itself tells us merely that the pair of them belonged to the same tradition of oral poetry, but certainly not that one knew and 'plagiarized' the other's work. With these passages the really significant fact is not the similarities which exist but the differences also to be found, for the differences enable us to assess the scope allowed each individual poet and make us realize that composition by formula and theme is neither rigid nor mechanical. Lord himself states that 'all singers use traditional material in a traditional way, but no two singers use exactly the same material in exactly the same way. . . . We can differentiate individual styles in the epic technique of oral verse-making'.[56] One feature of Hesiod's individual style, for example, is his preoccupation even in the Theogony with the law, which causes him to make his wise king function specifically in the law court (verses 81 ff.) and to add a group of Nereid names, unknown to Homer, which suggest wisdom in that same place (Themisto in verse 261).[57] But, to return to the main point, even if Homer's date were firmly established, there could be no question of our using coincidence of formulas and themes in order to determine Hesiod's *floruit*. We must wait until written poetry replaces oral composition, in other words, the advent of Archilochus, before such comparative evidence has any value for dating Hesiod.

Let me mention one example of what happens when Homer and Hesiod discuss the same kind of topic, their descriptions of Tartarus. Stokes gives a good idea of how scholars have wrangled in attempting to identify the earlier of the two descriptions; he personally decides in favour of the priority of the Theogony passage and regards my own preference for a common source as less probable 'especially as Tartarus does not seem to have been a common conception in the Epic period, being seldom mentioned in the Epics we possess'. But there was of course much epic poetry which has not survived, and Stokes himself says, only slightly before the words which I have quoted, that Hesiod's description of Tartarus 'is a "typical" scene of early poetry, which had a penchant for descriptions of "the other side" '.[58]

In the eighth book of the Iliad Zeus threatens to throw into Tartarus any god or goddess who persists in defying his command by aiding the Greeks or the Trojans (verses 10 ff.). Zeus emphasizes the great depth of misty Tartarus, refers to its gates of iron and bronze threshold, and describes it as being as much below Hades as heaven is from earth. In the Theogony Hesiod also describes Tartarus (verses 720 ff.): it is separated from the earth by as great a distance as divides heaven and earth. It takes a bronze anvil a full nine nights and days to pass down from heaven to earth, which it would reach only on the tenth; the same length of time is required for the anvil to continue its journey all the way to Tartarus. This gloomy place is enclosed in a wall of bronze, and there are doors likewise of bronze, provided by the god Poseidon, and a great threshold of bronze. Its depth is such that, even from within its gates, a man would struggle against the adverse winds a whole year to reach its bottom. The underworld is a loathsome place, and the gods certainly do not care for it, as both Homer and Hesiod tell us in a formulaic line which they share with only a minor variation (cf. Iliad xx, 65 and Theogony, 739 and 810). Hesiod locates Night and her children, Hypnos and Thanatos, in Tartarus (verses 744 and 758–9), and upon Hypnos and Thanatos the bright Sun with his rays never looks, either when mounting up to heaven or when descending back to earth (verses 759–61). In the Odyssey we learn of another region, the land and city of the Cimmerians, where the sun never shines and deadly night enshrouds wretched mortals (xi, 15–9).

Homer refers to Tartarus only to add weight to Zeus' threat, whereas Hesiod provides a full treatment of this theme. When the two descriptions are compared, we see both differences and similarities; the former surely preclude any possibility of direct imitation, whether it was Homer or Hesiod who was the borrower, while the latter are perfectly understandable in terms of a common repertoire of formulas and themes. Whenever either Homer or Hesiod had to describe the lower regions or anywhere else horribly dark, like the land of the Cimmerians, the standard theme automatically suggested a certain pattern of presentation and particular formulas. As a result we meet descriptions of Tartarus characterized by a basic similarity, but a similarity relieved, however, by variations of detail which reflect the individual treatments of the theme.

I said earlier that we must not forget that Homer and Hesiod are separated by the expanse of the Aegean Sea. Differences between Ionian and Boeotian epic poetry become evident when we begin to examine the mainland and Ionian versions of some of the Greek myths and the ways in which Homer and Hesiod handled their material.[59] Yet, at the same time, Homer and Hesiod share formulas and themes, and this must mean that they belong to what is fundamentally the same tradition of oral verse. Our tendency to draw a distinction between two schools of epic, one centred in Ionia and the other on the mainland of Greece, should not blind us to the fact that, while these two streams of poetry did exist, they have so much in common that their separation must have been quite recent and probably not earlier than the ninth-century date advocated by Webster. The tradition common to both Greek poets is one which stretches back to the Mycenaean period. I wish to stress their common inheritance, because, having now, I trust, adequately discussed the Near Eastern texts relevant to a study of Hesiod, and having attempted to associate their influence with certain periods of time, I think a final question appropriate: can we isolate the elements in the Theogony which are solely Greek and owe nothing to the Near East? This is rather like trying to establish the character of pure Roman religion, uncontaminated by Greek beliefs; in both cases foreign influence comes too early for the problem to be answerable. But we may be able to answer a modified form of question: can we isolate the elements in the Theogony which had become part of Greek tradition before epic poetry was divided into two streams? There are several ways in which this question may be tackled, and it is my intention to close the book with one which is not unrelated to what I have just been saying about comparable passages in Homer and Hesiod.

Is it possible to claim that whatever the two poets know and describe in similar language is Greek tradition in the sense that it goes back to the period before epic poetry among the Greeks had split into its two streams? This split should have occurred before the new wave of Near Eastern influence was carried from North Syria to Greece by the Euboeans or the Phoenicians, and if such tradition shows traces of Near Eastern influence, the influence must be older than the Dark Ages.[60] Notopoulos has said that 'whatever Homer and Hesiod share in common, be it diction or theme, is better accounted for by mutual borrowings from the survival of the Achaean tradition of oral poetry'.[61] To his list of diction and theme I would add a third category, namely foreign influence. If my argument is acceptable, the fact that Homer and Hesiod describe Tartarus in much the same terms means that here we are faced with a Greek tradition none of whose details, insofar as they are to be found in both the Homeric poems and the Theogony, may be referred to the influence of the Near East, unless that influence had already been felt while Mycenae remained strong. The conclusion can be verified by a quick look at the contents of the fifth tablet of Enuma Elish, the first part of which deals with the organization of the heavens and the earth, but not that of the lower regions. But Tartarus is perhaps of minor importance; much more interesting are references to the several kings of the gods, quarrels between the gods, and the attempts made to depose Zeus. What has Homer to say about these subjects, and to what extent does he employ formulas also known to Hesiod? Unfortunately, Homer offers disappointingly little in the way of comparative material, and what little there is comes mainly in the *Dios Apate* and the following book of the Iliad. A brief reference to Okeanos as the origin of the gods and later as the origin of all things (xiv, 201 and 246) and a quarrel between Okeanos and Tethys (verses 205–7) suggests the first pair, Tiamat and Apsu, of Enuma Elish (p. 34), but Hesiod, apart from making Tethys the consort of Okeanos in the Theogony (verse 337), ignores this idea. If both Homer and Hesiod knew of the Babylonian Epic of Creation, they used it quite differently. Homer mentions several incidents in the mythology of Zeus and Hera (xiv, 202–4 and 295–6, and xv, 18 ff.) about which Hesiod says nothing – but then he had no reason to say anything of them. We are still searching, therefore, for what is mentioned not by one only of the poets, but by both of them. What comes under this heading, and how alike is the language they employ? Homer makes a number of passing references to Kronos and the Titans in Tartarus (Iliad viii, 479–81; xiv, 203–4, 274, and 279; and xv, 225), and in the second of these Zeus is responsible for putting Kronos there. Verbal parallels are restricted to verse 851 of the Theogony, and, while I would argue that this motif goes back to the second millennium B.C. (p. 8), the fate of Tiamat's supporters in Enuma Elish appears to have enkindled fresh inspiration (p. 44). If the word Οὐρανίωνες in Iliad v, 898 refers to the imprisonment of the Titans, then Homer knew that the Titans were the sons of Ouranos. Catalogues are another traditional feature of Greek epic poetry and are, therefore, to be found in both poets, the most striking example of coincidence being their catalogues of the daughters of Nereus (Iliad xviii, 39 ff. and Theogony,

243 ff.). Homer mentions Typhoeus in the Iliad (ii, 782–3), but, for an account of Zeus in peril and needing an ally, we have to turn to an episode not included in the Theogony, the story of how Thetis rescued Zeus from his bonds and called in Briareos to help the king of the gods (i, 396–406). Like Hesiod, Homer was acquainted with the divine oath by Styx (xv, 37–8 and Theogony, 775 ff.) and Hypnos as the brother of Thanatos (xiv, 231 and Theogony, 756). Both poets personified Night (xiv, 259–61 and Theogony, 744 ff.) and appreciated the power of love (cf. xiv, 198–9 and 216–7, and Theogony, 120–2, 201, 205–6, and 224).[62]

If we add to the traditions available to both Homer and Hesiod those Near Eastern parallels which we have identified on texts dating from the second millennium B.C., we shall have some inkling of what was likely to have been at the disposal of the Greeks before contacts with the Orient were renewed. The Kingship in Heaven text (1400–1200 B.C.) tells of the successive dynasties of the gods and the sequence grandfather Heaven, father, and Storm-god son, and of the castration of Heaven by his successor. In the Song of Ullikummi the eventual king of the gods is matched against a monster who challenges his authority. This poem and the Ugaritic Epic of Baal (1400–1350 B.C.) show the young god relying on special weapons in order to vanquish his opponent. The cenotaph of Seti I (1300 B.C.) proves the existence of an Egyptian tradition which related the story of how Sky consumed her own children, an act resulting in a quarrel between Sky and Earth and their separation by the god Shu. If the material at the disposal of Greek poets was something like this, it underwent a startling transformation at the hands of Hesiod, the consequences of which we see in our text of the Theogony: it became embellished with catalogues and was organized into a series of dramatic episodes, all carefully balanced so as to give the poem its basic unity of structure. It was, moreover, no longer the story of the universe and the gods; it was now a glorious hymn of praise relating the exploits of a king of the gods, as just as he was terrible. In this respect its closest companions in Greek literature are the Homeric Hymns, but even closer is the picture of Zeus in the Theogony and that of Marduk in Enuma Elish, and it is to Babylonian tradition and the eighth century B.C. that we should resort if we wish to assess Hesiod's debt to the Near East.

We have travelled far in our effort to show that there is much more to be said about Hesiod and the Near East than we have been accustomed to suspect. The problem is intricate, and no one can hope to find all the answers; it will be a long time before we arrive at anything approaching final truth. For the present there is need of further evidence, which we may expect to derive from two sources, the specialized study, first, of Linear B and, secondly, of Near Eastern texts: a Linear B tablet may be found from which we have indisputable evidence of the Mycenaean ancestry of the sequence Ouranos, Kronos, and Zeus; there is certainly no lack of texts to keep Near Eastern scholars at work for many years to come, but these have to be studied, discussed, and then presented to an audience whose own knowledge in these highly technical fields of research is inevitably restricted. Given time, however, all this will be achieved, and the results may produce many surprises, for I am confident that we are just beginning to scratch the surface in our comparative studies. Like its predecessors in the field, this book is incomplete. But, though conscious of this and other imperfections, I still venture to offer it to its readers as worthy of their attention, if only as a hint of what the future, in some cases perhaps even the near future, may hold in store for us. The possibilities are as exciting as they are far-reaching.

NOTES TO THE INTRODUCTION

[1] The most comprehensive of these collections is that edited by J. B. Pritchard, *Ancient Near Eastern Texts relating to the Old Testament* (Princeton[2], 1955). *La Naissance du Monde* (Paris, 1959), the first volume in a new series entitled 'Sources Orientales', contains an extensive selection of creation myths in translation. Discussions of creation myths published recently range from S. G. F. Brandon's popular treatment in *Creation Legends of the Ancient Near East* (London, 1963) to Hans Schwabl's article 'Weltschöpfung' in *RE* suppl. bd. IX (Stuttgart, 1962).

[2] Cf. my article in *CQ* 6 (1956), pp. 198–206. I have examined the structure of the *prooemium* of the Theogony and the 'hymns' to Aphrodite, Styx, and Hekate in *SO* 33 (1957), pp. 37–47 and 34 (1958), pp. 5–14. Repetition in the Theogony has since been studied by C. Angier, *HSPh* 68 (1964), pp. 329–44.

[3] G. S. Kirk in *Hésiode et son Influence* (Entretiens sur l'Antiquité classique 7, Geneva, 1962), pp. 63–95.

NOTES TO CHAPTER I

[1] The myths are translated by Albrecht Goetze in *ANET*, pp. 120–5.

[2] F. Dornseiff, *AC* 6 (1937), pp. 246–7 (=*Antike und alter Orient* (Leipzig[2], 1959), pp. 55–6).

[3] M. P. Nilsson, *Geschichte der griechischen Religion* (Munich, 1941), 1, p. 486 n. 2.

[4] H. G. Güterbock, *Kumarbi* (Zürich-New York, 1946) and *AJA* 52 (1948), pp. 123–34.

[5] *Mythologies*, pp. 155 ff.

[6] *The Song of Ullikummi*, New Haven, 1952 (=*JCS* 5 (1951), pp. 135–61 and 6 (1952), pp. 8–42).

[7] *Kumarbi*, p. 112.

[8] See, however, *Kumarbi*, p. 102 and *AJA* 52 (1948), pp. 125 and 130.

[9] One solution has been proposed by F. Vian, *La Guerre des Géants* (Paris, 1952), pp. 181–3.

[10] R. D. Barnett in *Éléments*, pp. 148–9.

[11] E. A. Speiser, *JAOS* 62 (1942), p. 100 n. 14.

[12] Kirk and J. E. Raven, *The Presocratic Philosophers* (Cambridge, 1957), pp. 26–37.

[13] See chapter 2 n. 20.

[14] For the 'Former Gods' as a group of underworld deities, see O. R. Gurney, *Annals of Archaeology and Anthropology* 27 (1940), pp. 81–2.

[15] *Mythologies*, p. 171.

[16] T. B. L. Webster, *Minos* 4 (1956), pp. 112–3.

[17] C. Kardara, *AJA* 64 (1960), p. 354.

[18] For Atlas see A. Lesky, *AAWW* 87 (1950), pp. 148 ff. and *Saeculum* 6 (1955), pp. 47–8, and to rise in respect *Eranos* 52 (1954), pp. 14–5 and *Saeculum* 6 (1955), pp. 49–50.

[19] *ANET*, pp. 103–4.

[20] Gurney, *PBA* 1955, pp. 27–33 and *AS* 10 (1960), pp. 105–31.

[21] Cf. A. M. Frenkian, *Studia et Acta Orientalia* 4 (1962), pp. 91–4 on the Gilgamesh story and Homer.

[22] F. Worms, *Hermes* 81 (1953), pp. 29 ff., and M. C. Stokes, *Phronesis* 7 (1962), pp. 4 and 33–6.

[23] Goetze, *BASO* 79 (1940), pp. 32–3.

[24] *Mythologies*, p. 172.

[25] The Typhoeus myth is discussed by Vian in *Éléments*, pp. 17 ff., and by J. Fontenrose, *Python* (Berkeley, 1959), pp. 70 ff.

[26] Cf. Virgil's island *Inarime* in Aeneid ix, 716.

[27] See Vian, op. cit., pp. 21–2, and Fontenrose, op. cit., pp. 78–9.

[28] Cf. P. Guillon, *Le Bouclier d'Héraclès* (Aix, 1963), p. 89 n. 118. A desire to supply the Theogony with a Boeotian background has also produced the theory, argued by P. Mazon, *Hésiode* (Paris, 1928), pp. 21–4, and by B. A. van Groningen, *La Composition littéraire archaïque grecque* (Amsterdam², 1960), pp. 269–70, that a local festival of the goddess Hekate provided the occasion for the first performance of the Theogony.

[29] O. Eissfeldt, *Ras Schamra und Sanchunjaton* (Beiträge zur Religionsgeschichte des Altertums 4, Halle, 1939), pp. 112 ff. and 128 ff., and, for the passage under discussion here, 140–1.

[30] *ANET*, pp. 125–6.

[31] Cf. Ph. H. J. Houwink ten Cate, *The Luwian Population Groups of Lycia and Cilicia Aspera during the Hellenistic Period* (Leiden, 1961), pp. 208–9 and 211–4. Also of interest, although not directly relevant, is G. M. A. Hanfmann, *HSPh* 63 (1958), pp. 68 ff. on the story of Tylos and Masnes (Dionysiaca xxv, 451 ff.), the Epic of Gilgamesh, and the Anatolian myths.

[32] *Mythologies*, p. 152.

[33] *ANET*, p. 84.

[34] *ANET*, pp. 151–2 and 153 (=Driver, pp. 55 and 59). A new episode from the Baal Epic reveals that Anat's attitude towards Baal can be similarly capricious (C. Virolleaud, *CRAI* 1960, pp. 182–4).

[35] P. Perdrizet, *RHR* 105 (1932), pp. 193 ff. is a notable exception.

[36] Fontenrose, op. cit., p. 290, and C. J. Gadd, *The Cities of Babylonia* (*CAH*, fasc. 9, 1962), p. 19 n. 6.

[37] P. E. 1, 9, 20 ff. (=*FGH* 790 F 1–2).

[38] *ANET*, p. 141 (=Driver, p. 115). Sanchuniathon and this colophon are discussed by Eissfeldt, *Sanchunjaton von Berut und Ilumilku von Ugarit* (Beiträge zur Religionsgeschichte des Altertums 5, Halle, 1952), pp. 58 ff.

[39] P. E. 1, 10, 50 (=*FGH* 790 F 4). This passage is no. 61 and the Suda reference no. 47 in Kirk's chapter on Pherecydes in *The Presocratic Philosophers*.

[40] See Kirk in *The Presocratic Philosophers*, pp. 48–72, and M. L. West, *CQ* 13 (1963), pp. 157–72.

[41] E. Laroche, *JCS* 6 (1952), pp. 115–23.

[42] *ANET*, p. 393.

[43] Goetze examines the population of Cilicia in the second and first millennia B. C. in *JCS* 16 (1962), pp. 48–58.

[44] Güterbock, *CHM* 2 (1954–55), pp. 383–94.

[45] Speiser, *CHM* 1 (1953), pp. 311–27. I. McNeill, *AS* 13 (1963), pp. 237–42 shows that our Hittite texts owe their metre to Mesopotamia.

[46] Virolleaud, *CRAI* 1962, p. 93; see also the comments by C. F. A. Schaeffer, *CRAI* 1963, pp. 153–5. On the absence of Greek names at Ugarit but other evidence which suggests West Semitic influence on Crete and the Mycenaeans, see M. C. Astour, *JNES* 23 (1964), pp. 193–201.

[47] M. H. Pope, *El in the Ugaritic Texts*, suppl. to *Vetus Testamentum* 2 (Leiden, 1955), pp. 30–2 and 93–4.

[48] Damascius, de princ. 124 b (=Kirk no. 51).

[49] Kirk, op. cit., pp. 58 and 71.

[50] *ANET*, p. 137 (=Driver, p. 91).

⁵¹ Pope, op. cit., pp. 61–81.

⁵² Driver, pp. 121–5 translates this myth.

⁵³ Pherecydes as reported by Proclus, in Tim. 32C (=Kirk no. 55), and Philo by Eusebius, P. E. 1, 10, 1.

⁵⁴ According to the author of the Titanomachia, the father of Ouranos was Aither (Allen, fr. 1).

⁵⁵ See Eissfeldt (n. 29).

⁵⁶ Thus Schwabl in *Éléments*, p. 46.

⁵⁷ *ANET*, p. 137 (=Driver, p. 87).

⁵⁸ *Kumarbi*, pp. 10–2 and *Mythologies*, pp. 161–4.

NOTES TO CHAPTER II

¹ Stokes, *Phronesis* 7 (1962), pp. 36–7 argues convincingly for the retention of these lines; see also H. Erbse, *Philologus* 108 (1964), pp. 8 ff.

² Cf. Schwabl, *Hermes* 90 (1962), pp. 122–3.

³ Cf. Schwabl, *Serta Philologica Aenipontana* 7–8 (1961), pp. 72–84.

⁴ Mazon, *Hésiode*, pp. 13–4. The discussion reported in *Hésiode et son Influence*, pp. 98 ff. shows that the argument continues.

⁵ *ANET*, p. 131 (= Driver, pp. 81 and 83).

⁶ F. M. Cornford, *The Unwritten Philosophy* (Cambridge, 1950), pp. 95 ff.

⁷ *Principium Sapientiae* (Cambridge, 1952), pp. 202 ff. My quotation is taken from pp. 248–9.

⁸ See G. Steiner's dissertation *Der Sukzessionsmythos in Hesiods 'Theogonie' und ihren orientalischen Parallelen* (Hamburg, 1958), pp. 99 ff.

⁹ See Güterbock's note (*Kumarbi*, pp. 36–7) on the Kingship in Heaven text col. II, 4. In *Naissance*, p. 157 M. Vieyra falls back on the lame explanation that, if the Kumarbi myth and the Song of Ullikummi ignore Marduk so pointedly, it is because Hurrian borrowing dates in the main from the period before the First Dynasty of Babylon.

¹⁰ Unless otherwise noted, I quote the translation of Enuma Elish by Alexander Heidel, *The Babylonian Genesis* (Phoenix Books, 1963). Speiser translates Enuma Elish in *ANET*, pp. 60–72. For the fifth tablet I have used B. Landsberger and J. V. Kinnier Wilson, *JNES* 20 (1961), pp. 154–79. Gurney translates passages from the fourth, first, and sixth tablets which have been supplemented by the Sultantepe finds in *AS* 2 (1952), pp. 27–34. W. G. Lambert of the University of Birmingham has most generously allowed me to read part of the manuscript of his forthcoming edition of Babylonian creation texts.

¹¹ Eudemus of Rhodes fr. 150 (Wehrli).

¹² Gurney, op. cit., p. 28.

¹³ Marduk is the person referred to in iv, 67–8, and the gods of the following two lines are the supporters of Marduk.

¹⁴ H. Schmökel, *RAA* 53 (1959), pp. 183–204.

¹⁵ For the present see L. Matouš, *Archiv Orientální* 29 (1961), pp. 30–4. W. von Soden, *Mitteilungen der deutschen Orient-Gesellschaft* 85 (1953), pp. 14–26 discusses the problem of arranging our Babylonian texts in a chronological sequence, while Lambert sketches the development of Mesopotamian thought and literature in the introductory chapter of his *Babylonian Wisdom Literature* (Oxford, 1960), pp. 1–20.

¹⁶ W. W. Hallo, *IEJ* 12 (1962), pp. 16 ff.

¹⁷ The Mesopotamian background of the Kumarbi myth is examined by Speiser in *JAOS* 62 (1942), pp. 98–102.

[18] Gurney, *PBA* 1955, p. 26. That the suggestion is not a new one may be seen from S. Langdon, *The Babylonian Epic of Creation* (Oxford, 1923), pp. 17 ff. To the translation of the Myth of Zu in *ANET*, pp. 111–3 and 515–6 and the bibliography cited there should now be added E. Reiner, *RAA* 51 (1957), pp. 107–10.

[19] The myth is translated by Heidel, op. cit., pp. 141–3.

[20] Verse 119 of the Theogony forms part of the relative clause which begins in 118, Olympus and Tartarus representing the top and bottom respectively, as in verses 680–2. See also Stokes, *Phronesis* 8 (1963), pp. 1–4.

[21] Lambert translates the text in a joint article by himself and the author of this book in *Kadmos* 4 (1965), pp. 64–72. On the incest theme see F. Dirlmeier, *Der Mythos von König Oedipus* (Mainz², 1964), pp. 21 ff.

[22] Some scholars, two of whom are Paley in the last and Kirk in this century, have argued that a part of the original text of the Theogony where the dethronement of Kronos was described has been lost. Diodorus, in his account of Cretan tradition, records that some claimed that, after Kronos' death and elevation to heaven, Zeus became king 'not having prevailed over his father by force, but in accordance with usage and justice, having been deemed worthy of the honour' (5, 70, 1).

[23] Landsberger and Kinnier Wilson, op. cit., pp. 161 and 163.

[24] R. Merkelbach, *SIFC* 27–8 (1956), pp. 289–90, and Walcot, *SO* 38 (1963), pp. 15–6.

[25] Full details of critical discussion of the description of Tartarus are to be found in the article by Stokes (see n. 1), pp. 2–33.

[26] Berossus, *FGH* 680 F 1; Eudemus of Rhodes fr. 150 (Wehrli).

[27] Lambert, *RAA* 53 (1959), pp. 121–2.

[28] Landsberger and Kinnier Wilson, op. cit., p. 163.

[29] J. Kroll, *SIFC* 27–8 (1956), pp. 181–91.

[30] Webster, *Greek Art and Literature 700–530 B.C.* (London, 1959), p. 17 n. 15.

[31] F. Gössmann, *Das Era-Epos*, Würzburg.

[32] *Mythologies*, pp. 127–35.

[33] Cornford, *Principium Sapientiae*, pp. 88 ff.

[34] Lambert, *JCS* 11 (1957), pp. 1–14 and 112, and *Babylonian Wisdom Literature*, pp. 13–4. See also the list of wise men discussed by J. van Dijk in H. Lenzen, *Vorläufiger Bericht über die Ausgrabungen in Uruk-Warka* 18, Winter 1959–60 (Berlin, 1962), pp. 44 ff., and Hallo, *JAOS* 83 (1963), pp. 174–6.

[35] Lambert, *JCS* 16 (1962), pp. 59–77.

[36] Lambert, *AOF* 18 (1957–58), pp. 396–8 and 400; see also van Dijk's comment (p. 51 n. 130) on line thirteen of the Uruk list.

[37] I quote Lambert's translation of the fifth tablet in *Iraq* 24 (1962), pp. 119–25.

[38] A. L. Oppenheim, 'The Interpretation of Dreams in the ancient Near East', *Transactions of the American Philosophical Society* n.s. 46, 3 (1956), pp. 193–4 and 354.

[39] R. Anthes, *JNES* 16 (1957), pp. 185–90.

NOTES TO CHAPTER III

[1] Heidel, *The Babylonian Genesis*, pp. 118–22, and V. Maag, *Asiatische Studien* 8 (1954), pp. 85–106 discuss the Babylonian accounts of the creation of mankind. My own description of these myths owes much to the section on the creation of man in Lambert's forthcoming edition of Babylonian creation texts. A summary of a paper by Lambert on this subject appears in *Compte Rendu de la XIième Rencontre Assyriologique Internationale* 1962 (Leiden, 1964), pp. 101–2.

[2] T. Jacobsen, *JNES* 5 (1946), pp. 134–7.

[3] This text is translated by Heidel, op. cit., pp. 68–71.

[4] Lambert, *Babylonian Wisdom Literature*, p. 89 (= *ANET*, p. 440). On the technique involved, see R. Amiran, *BASO* 167 (1962), pp. 23–5.

[5] Lambert, op. cit., p. 59 (= *ANET*, p. 437).

[6] *ANET*, pp. 74, 165, and 180.

[7] Heidel, op. cit., pp. 62–3.

[8] Cf. S. N. Kramer, *Sumerian Mythology* (New York², 1961), pp. 68–72, *History begins at Sumer* (London², 1961), pp. 161–4, and *The Sumerians* (Chicago, 1963), pp. 149–51.

[9] J. Laessøe, *BO* 13 (1956), pp. 90–102. Heidel, op. cit., p. 67 (= *ANET*, pp. 99–100) translates the relevant part of the Epic. An improved text with a German translation of the first tablet is published by von Soden, *Orientalia* 26 (1957), pp. 306–15.

[10] Güterbock, *Kumarbi*, p. 21 and *The Song of Ullikummi*, pp. 6–7.

[11] Güterbock, *Kumarbi*, p. 11 and *Mythologies*, p. 163.

[12] O. Lendle, *Die 'Pandorasage' bei Hesiod* (Würzburg, 1957), and G. Fink's dissertation *Pandora und Epimetheus* (Erlangen) give full bibliographical details. See also E. Heitsch, *RhM* 106 (1963), pp. 1–15.

[13] This part of the Theogony is analysed by H. and A. Thornton, *Time and Style* (London, 1962), pp. 14–6.

[14] West, *CQ* 11 (1961), pp. 137–8.

[15] Such is the opinion of E. Vandvik, *The Prometheus of Hesiod and Aeschylus* (Oslo, 1943), pp. 8 ff. and *SO* 24 (1945), p. 159.

[16] W. Nicolai, *Hesiods Erga, Beobachtungen zum Aufbau* (Heidelberg, 1964), pp. 25 ff. examines the structure of Hesiod's narrative.

[17] *Hermes* 89 (1961), p. 250. On bronze and magic see G. Germain, *Genèse de l'Odyssée* (Paris, 1954), pp. 153 ff.

[18] Stokes, *Phronesis* 7 (1962), p. 9.

[19] H. Wagenvoort, *Studies in Roman Literature, Culture and Religion* (Leiden, 1956), pp. 102–31.

[20] I imagine that the phrase 'to supply human voice and strength' (verses 61–2) does not mean more than 'to make a living mortal', and that we are misguided to see an inconsistency between Hephaistos being ordered to provide αὐδή and Hermes later equipping Pandora with φωνή (verses 79–80); cf. the same expression in Iliad xviii, 419–20 and the use of the adjective αὐδήεις to distinguish mortals from deities in Theogony, 142 b and Odyssey v, 334–5.

[21] P. E. 1, 10, 7 and 1, 10, 11 (= *FGH* 790 F 2).

[22] A. M. Badawi, *Der Gott Chnum* (Glückstadt, 1937) considers the meaning of the name, representations, and cult centres of the god Khnum; see also S. Sauneron and J. Yoyotte, *Naissance*, pp. 71–4.

[23] The reliefs are described and illustrated by E. Naville, *The Temple of Deir el Bahari* (London), Part II (1897), pp. 12–8 and plates 46–55, and Part III (1898), pp. 1–9 and plates 56–64, and by M. Werbrouck, *Le Temple d'Hatshepsout à Deir el Bahari* (Brussels, 1949), pp. 49–65. I quote the translation of the inscriptions by J. H. Breasted, *Ancient Records of Egypt* II (Chicago, 1906), pp. 75–100. The new study by H. Brunner, *Die Geburt des Gottkönigs* (Ägyptologische Abhandlungen 10, Wiesbaden, 1964) includes translations in German of the birth inscriptions from Deir el-Bahari and Luxor and illustrations of the Luxor birth scenes. See also F. Daumas, *Les Mammisis des Temples égyptiens* (Paris, 1958), pp. 61–3 and 411–4.

[24] Cf. Brunner, op. cit., pp. 42–4 (Deir el-Bahari) and 45–6 (Luxor).

[25] The tale is translated by A. Erman, *The Literature of the Ancient Egyptians* (London, 1927), pp. 36–47.

²⁶ See S. N. Marinatos, *Studies presented to David M. Robinson*, 1 (St. Louis, 1951), pp. 129 ff.

²⁷ Daumas, *RHR* 149 (1956), pp. 1–17.

²⁸ Cf. Brunner, op. cit., p. 61.

²⁹ See, however, Brunner, op. cit., p. 68.

³⁰ Here, as elsewhere, I refer those of my readers who desire detailed accounts of Egyptian deities and concepts to the articles in H. Bonnet, *Reallexikon der ägyptischen Religionsgeschichte* (Berlin, 1952).

³¹ Cf. Antiphanes fr. 52 (Edmonds) τροχοῦ ῥυμαῖσι τευκτὸν κοιλοσώματον κύτος/πλαστὸν ἐκ γαίης (verses 2–3).

³² Cf. the dates suggested by R. A. Higgins, *BICS* 4 (1957), pp. 27–41 and *ABSA* 52 (1957), pp. 42–57, and by Clark Hopkins, *AJA* 66 (1962), pp. 182–4.

³³ Cf. I. Trencsényi-Waldapfel, *Acta Ethnographica* 4 (1955), p. 106.

³⁴ For the coronation of the pharaoh see H. Frankfort, *Kingship and the Gods* (Chicago, 1948), pp. 105–9, and H. W. Fairman in *Myth, Ritual, and Kingship* (Oxford, 1958), pp. 78 ff.

³⁵ G. Posener, *De la Divinité du Pharaon* (Paris, 1960), pp. 37–9.

³⁶ G. Widengren, *Myth, Ritual, and Kingship*, pp. 183–9.

³⁷ Virolleaud, *CRAI* 1962, p. 95, and Schaeffer, *CRAI* 1962, pp. 204–5 (= *AArchSyr* 13 (1963), p. 133).

³⁸ For the whole subject of direct contact between Mycenae and Egypt one should consult A. W. Persson, *New Tombs at Dendra near Midea* (Lund, 1943), pp. 176–96, and for paintings in Egyptian tombs, including that of Senmut, Hatshepsut's great minister, which depict Minoan-Mycenaeans, F. Schachermeyr, *Das minoische Kultur des alten Kreta* (Stuttgart, 1964), pp. 112–5. Danaos is made a fleeing Hyksos by G. Huxley, *Crete and the Luwians* (Oxford, 1961), pp. 36–7, and by F. H. Stubbings, *The Rise of Mycenaean Civilization* (*CAH*, fasc. 18, 1963), pp. 11–4.

³⁹ Marinatos, *Festschrift Bernhard Schweitzer* (Stuttgart, 1954), pp. 11–8; cf. also *ABSA* 46 (1951), pp. 102–16. It is important to note that, when the Mycenaeans appear to adopt a theme from Egyptian art, we need not suppose that the symbolism of the theme was retained (cf. S. I. Charitonides, *AD* 16 (1960), pp. 84–90).

⁴⁰ Nilsson, *The Minoan-Mycenaean Religion* (Lund², 1950), pp. 426–43; cf. F. Matz, *Göttererscheinung und Kultbild im minoischen Kreta* (Akad. der Wiss. & der Lit. in Mainz, Abh. der Geistes- & Sozialwiss. Kl. 1958, 7), pp. 18–27, Schachermeyr, op. cit., pp. 170–3, and J. P. Nauert, *AK* 8 (1965), pp. 91–8.

⁴¹ L. R. Palmer, *The Interpretation of Mycenaean Greek Texts* (Oxford, 1963), pp. 338–63.

⁴² W. K. C. Guthrie, *BICS* 6 (1959), p. 42.

⁴³ Frankfort, op. cit., pp. 57–8 (Egypt) and 309–12 (Mesopotamia).

⁴⁴ Germain, op. cit., pp. 185–7.

⁴⁵ *ANET*, pp. 394–6. The Plague Prayers are discussed by Gurney in *Myth, Ritual, and Kingship*, pp. 110–2.

⁴⁶ *ANET*, p. 417.

⁴⁷ *ANET*, p. 415.

⁴⁸ *ANET*, pp. 147, 148, and 149 (= Driver, pp. 41, 43, and 47).

⁴⁹ For *basileus* and for the skilled man and patron god see Webster, *A Companion to Homer* (London, 1962), pp. 457–8 and 459–60, and for 'Mother Theia' H. J. Rose, ibid., pp. 474–5, and Palmer, op. cit., p. 257.

⁵⁰ M. Ventris and J. Chadwick, *Documents in Mycenaean Greek* (Cambridge, 1956), pp. 305–6.

⁵¹ Nilsson, op. cit., pp. 459–60 and 60 ff., and R. W. Hutchinson, *Prehistoric Crete* (Pelican, 1962), pp. 201–3. Hesiod's references to Crete are of a special importance, since it has been claimed that the island forms a link in the chain of transmission between the Hurrians and the Theogony (cf. U. Hölscher, *Hermes* 81 (1953), pp. 404–11, and F. B. Anderson, *CJ* 50 (1954), pp. 131–8). In a privately circulated newsletter, dated 1 November 1962, C. H. Gordon claims that two Hurrian names occur in the Minoan texts from Hagia Triada; cf. also M. L. and H. Erlenmeyer, *Orientalia* 33 (1964), pp. 199 ff.

⁵² Cf. R. F. Willetts, *Cretan Cults and Festivals* (London, 1962), p. 113. See also J. Wiesner, *JDAI* 74 (1959), pp. 48–51 on Works and Days, 524.

⁵³ *ANET*, p. 378.

⁵⁴ *ANET*, pp. 378–9.

⁵⁵ My quotations are taken from Frankfort, op. cit., pp. 150, 149, 102, and 150. The Apophis text is translated in *ANET*, pp. 6–7. Cf. the interpretation of Pindar, Pyth. 1 proposed by J. Trumpf, *Hermes* 86 (1958), pp. 129–57.

⁵⁶ The temple programme for the New Year festival at Babylon is translated in *ANET*, pp. 331–4. A summary of Lambert's views on what took place in the *Akitu* house will be found in *Iraq* 25 (1963), pp. 189–90.

⁵⁷ Brandon, *Myth, Ritual, and Kingship*, p. 290.

⁵⁸ A. N. Marlow, *BRL* 43 (1961), pp. 373–402. A. B. Lord in *A Companion to Homer*, pp. 197–205 discusses the ritual and magical origin of epic. On Mycenaean festivals see Palmer, op. cit., pp. 250–68, and on the god Dionysos in the Linear B tablets J. Puhvel in *Mycenaean Studies* (Madison, 1964), pp. 161–70.

⁵⁹ Convenient accounts of this subject are S. Morenz, *La Religion égyptienne* (Paris, 1962), pp. 211 ff., and Brandon, *Creation Legends of the Ancient Near East*, pp. 14 ff., while selections of the relevant texts are included in *ANET*, pp. 3 ff. and in *Naissance*, pp. 19 ff.

⁶⁰ The standard translation and commentary on the Pyramid Texts is that by S. A. B. Mercer, *The Pyramid Texts* (New York, 1952).

⁶¹ Translated by A. de Buck in Frankfort, *The Cenotaph of Seti I at Abydos* (London, 1933), p. 83; see also Anthes, *Mythologies*, pp. 64–5.

⁶² The first part of the story is translated in *ANET*, pp. 23–5, and the complete text by Erman, op. cit., pp. 150–61.

NOTES TO CHAPTER IV

¹ I discuss Hesiod and the didactic literature of the Near East in *REG* 75 (1962), pp. 13–36; see also Nicolai, *Hesiods Erga, Beobachtungen zum Aufbau*, pp. 190 ff.

² Compare throughout my analysis of the structure of the Works and Days in *REG* 74 (1961), pp. 1–19. Much is to be learnt from A. Masaracchia, *Helikon* 1 (1961), pp. 217–44; W. J. Verdenius, *Hésiode et son Influence*, pp. 111 ff.; H. Diller, *Die dichterische Form von Hesiods Erga* (Akad. der Wiss. & der Lit. in Mainz, Abh. der Geistes- & Sozialwiss. Kl. 1962, 2); K. Kumaniecki, *BICS* 10 (1963), pp. 79–96; and the book by Nicolai cited in n. 1. See also F. Krafft, *Vergleichende Untersuchungen zu Homer und Hesiod* (Göttingen, 1963), pp. 86 ff.

³ See S. E. Bassett, *The Poetry of Homer* (Berkeley, 1938), pp. 120–8 for this pattern in Homer and Hebrew poetry.

⁴ Verdenius, op. cit., p. 117.

⁵ Kramer, *Sumerian Mythology*, pp. 64–8, *History begins at Sumer*, pp. 153–6, and *The Sumerians*, pp. 160–2.

⁶ J. Gwyn Griffiths, *JHI* 17 (1956), pp. 115–9.

[7] *REG* 74 (1961), pp. 6–7; cf. also J. P. Vernant, *RHR* 157 (1960), pp. 21 ff.

[8] A full and up-to-date bibliography of recent publications on Egyptian wisdom texts is given by J. Leclant in *Sagesses*, pp. 18–26. Wilson translates the majority of these texts, though sometimes with omissions, in *ANET*, pp. 412 ff. Texts, both published and unpublished, are listed by Posener, *Revue d'Égyptologie* 6 (1951), pp. 27 ff., who mentions precepts (nos. 54 and 56) in the form of prohibitions where each maxim begins with the same word (cf. Works and Days, 707 ff.).

[9] A complete translation in French is provided by Z. Žaba, *Les Maximes de Ptahhotep* (Prague, 1956), pp. 69–105.

[10] Posener and J. Sainte Fare Garnot, *Sagesses*, pp. 153–7.

[11] I quote the translation of the full text by F. Ll. Griffith, *JEA* 12 (1926), pp. 195–225.

[12] S. R. K. Glanville, *Catalogue of Demotic Papyri in the British Museum* 2, *The Instructions of 'Onchsheshonqy* (London, 1955).

[13] Glanville, op. cit., p. xv; cf. B. Gemser, *Congress Volume Oxford* 1959, suppl. to *Vetus Testamentum* 7 (Leiden, 1960), pp. 115–7.

[14] *JNES* 21 (1962), pp. 215–9.

[15] Glanville, op. cit., pp. xii and 65–6.

[16] *ANET*, p. 432.

[17] *ANET*, pp. 427–30. For the full text see A. Cowley, *Aramaic Papyri of the Fifth Century B.C.* (Oxford, 1923), pp. 220–6.

[18] Reiner, *Orientalia* 30 (1961), pp. 7–9; cf. the Uruk list of wise men published by van Dijk (see chapter two n. 34). Parallels between the Works and Days and the Words of Ahiqar are assessed by M. Riemschneider, *Von Olympia bis Ninive im Zeitalter Homers* (Leipzig, 1963), pp. 109 ff.

[19] For the Sumerian animal fable see E. I. Gordon, *JCS* 12 (1958), pp. 1–21 and 43–72, and *Festschrift V. V. Struve* (Moscow, 1962), pp. 226–49. M. Nøjgaard, *La Fable antique* 1 (Copenhagen, 1964), pp. 433–41 discusses Near Eastern and Greek fables and the links between them.

[20] Lambert, *Babylonian Wisdom Literature*, pp. 110–5.

[21] Lambert, op. cit., pp. 92–5, and Kramer, *Iraq* 25 (1963), pp. 174–5.

[22] J. Nougayrol, *Sagesses*, pp. 47–50 and *CRAI* 1963, pp. 132–42.

[23] Lambert, op. cit., pp. 96–107 (= *ANET*, pp. 426–7).

[24] Lambert, op. cit., pp. 121–38 (= *ANET*, pp. 387–9).

[25] R. Pettazzoni, *The All-Knowing God* (London, 1956), pp. 145 ff. and 155 ff.

[26] J. W. B. Barns, *Five Ramesseum Papyri* (Oxford, 1956), pp. 1–2. The Story of the Eloquent Peasant is translated in *ANET*, pp. 407–10.

[27] Kramer, *Sumerian Mythology*, pp. 79–82, *History begins at Sumer*, pp. 242–4, and *The Sumerians*, pp. 151–3.

[28] Kramer, *History begins at Sumer*, pp. 109–13 and *The Sumerians*, pp. 105–9 and, for a translation of the text, 340–2.

[29] *The Sumerians*, pp. 246–8.

[30] G. Nussbaum, *CQ* 10 (1960), p. 215 n. 5.

[31] *ANET*, p. 320. On the date and the purpose of the Gezer Calendar see S. Talmon, *JAOS* 83 (1963), p. 177.

[32] On the Meleager story see M. M. Willcock, *CQ* 14 (1964), pp. 147 ff.

[33] Diller, op. cit., pp. 15 ff.

[34] Details of the myth are given by R. T. Rundle Clark, *Myth and Symbol in Ancient Egypt* (London, 1959), pp. 103 ff.

[35] J. Friedrich, *Zeitschrift für Assyriologie* 49 (1950), pp. 215–25 (translation) and 242–6 (commentary).

[36] W. R. Dawson, *JEA* 12 (1926), pp. 260–4.

³⁷ S. Weinstock, *JHS* 69 (1949), pp. 57–9, and G. Thomson, *Studies in Ancient Greek Society* 2, *The First Philosophers* (London, 1955), pp. 111–4.

³⁸ E. Gjerstad, *Opuscula Atheniensia* 1 (Lund, 1953), pp. 187–91.

³⁹ West, *CQ* 11 (1961), p. 140. The latest study of the Days is that by F. Solmsen, *TAPhA* 94 (1963), pp. 293–320.

NOTES TO CHAPTER V

¹ G. Murray, *A History of Ancient Greek Literature* (London, 1897), pp. 6–7 and 53–5.

² Dornseiff, *Philologus* 89 (1934), p. 399 (= *Antike und alter Orient*, p. 75); cf. also Krafft, *Vergleichende Untersuchungen zu Homer und Hesiod*, pp. 92 ff.

³ Cf. my article in *SO* 38 (1963), pp. 5 ff.

⁴ Ephorus, *FGH* 70 F 100.

⁵ K. J. Beloch, *Griechische Geschichte* (Strassburg², 1912), 1, 1, p. 312 n. 1.

⁶ Archilochus A 17 (Lasserre).

⁷ T. J. Dunbabin, *The Western Greeks* (Oxford, 1948), pp. 3–8 discusses the foundation of Cyme.

⁸ As for the reason, land or trade, which caused the site to be colonized, see R. M. Cook, *Historia* 11 (1962), pp. 113–4.

⁹ W. G. Forrest, *Historia* 6 (1957), pp. 171–3.

¹⁰ The evidence, literary and archaeological, and its significance for absolute dates are assessed by Dunbabin, op. cit., pp. 435–71. C. G. Starr, *The Origins of Greek Civilization* (London, 1962), p. 228 n. 5 lists the various dates (from 800 to 725 B.C.) advanced for the foundation of Cyme. For the inadequacies of our evidence see J. Ducat, *BCH* 86 (1962), pp. 165–84; the Thucydidean chronology is defended by A. J. Graham, *Colony and Mother City in Ancient Greece* (Manchester, 1964), p. 221 n. 2.

¹¹ Kirk, *Hésiode et son Influence*, pp. 63–4, and Starr, op. cit., pp. 268 and 270–1.

¹² Cf. R. M. Cook, *CQ* 31 (1937), pp. 204–14, and J. L. Myres, *JHS* 61 (1941), pp. 17–38.

¹³ See Webster, *From Mycenae to Homer* (London, 1958), pp. 168–77.

¹⁴ R. Hampe, *Die Gleichnisse Homers und die Bildkunst seiner Zeit* (Tübingen, 1952), pp. 27 ff.

¹⁵ K. Friis Johansen, *Ajas und Hektor* (Hist. Filos. Medd. Dan. Vid. Selsk. 39, 4, Copenhagen, 1961). Cf. also H. Metzger, *REG* 77 (1964), pp. 116–8.

¹⁶ With the exception of three late ivories from Enkomi, the conflict between a fabulous beast and an anthropomorphic opponent does not form part of the repertoire of either the Minoan or the Mycenaean artist (see M. A. V. Gill, *BICS* 10 (1963), p. 1). H. L. Lorimer, *ABSA* 37 (1936–37), pp. 172–86 considers the Near Eastern background of a Protocorinthian aryballos (c. 680 B.C.) on which Zeus fights a horse-bodied adversary; as to the identity of Zeus' foe, see the bibliography cited by Vian, *La Guerre des Géants*, pp. 10–2.

¹⁷ R. J. H. Jenkins in *Perachora* 1 (Oxford, 1940), no. 183 (pp. 231–2). A better picture of the plaque will be found in an article on Astarte plaques by P. J. Riis, *Berytus* 9 (1948–49), plate xix, 1.

¹⁸ W. Sale, *TAPhA* 92 (1961), p. 515.

¹⁹ The vase is published by G. E. Mylonas, *The Protoattic Amphora of Eleusis* (in Greek), Athens, 1957.

²⁰ Cf. P. Courbin, *BCH* 79 (1955), pp. 37–42.

²¹ Mylonas, op. cit., pp. 102 and, for general conclusions, 115–6.

²² Mylonas, op. cit., pp. 112–3.

[23] M. Ervin, *AD* 18 (1963), pp. 37–75.

[24] *Archiloque* (Entretiens sur l'Antiquité classique 10, Geneva, 1964), plate iv offers a superb illustration of this scene.

[25] F. Brommer, *JRGZ* 8 (1961), pp. 72–3.

[26] For the date of Archilochus see J. Pouilloux, *Archiloque*, pp. 7 ff., and for Archilochus as a 'transitional' poet D. L. Page, ibid., pp. 119–63.

[27] Cf. Alcaeus fr. 347 (Lobel-Page) and Works and Days, 582–9.

[28] Webster, *Greek Art and Literature 700–530 B.C.*, p. 30. I number the fragments of Archilochus in accordance with F. Lasserre's Budé edition of the poet, as this includes the new Parian inscription (A 11a), on which now see A. Kambylis, *Hermes* 91 (1963), pp. 129–50.

[29] Lasserre, *Les Épodes d'Archiloque* (Paris, 1950), pp. 50–1 and 287–300.

[30] The Muses of Helicon are discussed by van Groningen, *AC* 17 (1948), pp. 287–96.

[31] Cf. A. D. Ure, *JHS* 49 (1929), pp. 160–71 on local pottery from sixth-century Boeotia associated with a famous shrine, which supplied it with both subject-matter and a market.

[32] J. M. Birmingham, *AS* 11 (1961), pp. 185–95.

[33] Aristotle fr. 611, 37 (Rose), and Pollux 9, 83.

[34] Huxley, *GRBS* 2 (1959), pp. 85–99; cf. E. Akurgal, *AJA* 66 (1962), pp. 372–3, who denies the importance of the Phrygians as middlemen between the Greeks and the Orient. Cf. also Akurgal in *Le Rayonnement des Civilisations grecque et romaine sur les Cultures périphériques* (Paris, 1965), pp. 467–74, and R. Young, ibid., pp. 481–5.

[35] Akurgal, *Anatolia* 1 (1956), pp. 11–4 reports the little that is known of Cyme archaeologically.

[36] Cf. Webster, *From Mycenae to Homer*, pp. 177–8, who approves a suggestion made by Lorimer that Hesiod received his poetic education in Athens. For direct contact between Attica and the Levant see Hanfmann, *Hesperia* 31 (1962), pp. 236–7.

[37] S. Benton, *ABSA* 35 (1934–35), p. 114 n. 1.

[38] Forrest, op. cit., pp. 160–4; cf. Graham, op. cit., p. 222 n. 3.

[39] E. Friedl, *Vasilika, a Village in Modern Greece* (New York, 1962), pp. 12 and 36.

[40] L. H. Jeffery, *The Local Scripts of Archaic Greece* (Oxford, 1961), pp. 91–2 and 94, select catalogue nos. 2, 3 a–e, 5, 6, and 9.

[41] Dunbabin, *The Greeks and their Eastern Neighbours* (London, 1957), pp. 24 ff., and J. Boardman, *The Greeks Overseas* (Pelican, 1964), pp. 57 ff. are excellent introductions to the general subject of the Greeks in the East.

[42] L. Woolley, *A Forgotten Kingdom* (Pelican, 1953), pp. 172–88.

[43] Boardman, *ABSA* 52 (1957), pp. 5 ff. and 24–7, and *The Greeks Overseas*, pp. 62–70.

[44] Boardman, *AS* 9 (1959), pp. 163–9.

[45] J. Du Plat Taylor, *Iraq* 21 (1959), pp. 62–92.

[46] A. R. Burn, *The Lyric Age of Greece* (London, 1960), pp. 49–52 sketches relations between Greeks and Assyrians during the period 750 to 690 B.C. The Greek pottery from Tarsus, as reported by Hanfmann in *The Aegean and the Near East* (Locust Valley, N.Y., 1956), pp. 165–84, is to be compared with the evidence from Al Mina.

[47] In addition to Du Plat Taylor (n. 45), see Birmingham, *AJA* 67 (1963), pp. 15–42 and *PalEQ* 1963, pp. 80–112.

[48] Riis, *AArchSyr* 8–9 (1958–59), pp. 128–30; 10 (1960), pp. 123 ff.; and 11–12 (1961–62), pp. 137–40.

[49] Thus Jeffery, op. cit., pp. 5–21, and R. M. Cook and A. G. Woodhead, *AJA* 63 (1959), p. 178.

[50] E. D. Phillips, *JHS* 73 (1953), pp. 55–6.

[51] A. A. Trever, *CPh* 19 (1924), p. 165.

[52] Hampe, *Frühe griechische Sagenbilder in Böotien* (Athens, 1936), p. 55; cf. also Guillon *La Béotie antique* (Paris, 1948), p. 27, and J. A. Notopoulos, *HSPh* 68 (1964), pp. 25–7.

[53] Cf. Notopoulos, op. cit., p. 38, 'Let it be clearly understood that one of the results of our increasing knowledge of oral poetry is that it is a genre of literature least subject to evolutionary concepts of development'.

[54] Krafft, op. cit., p. 119.

[55] Lord, *The Singer of Tales* (Cambridge, Mass., 1960), pp. 48–50.

[56] Lord, op. cit., p. 63.

[57] Walcot, *SO* 38 (1963), pp. 10–6.

[58] Stokes, *Phronesis* 7 (1962), pp. 5–6 and 3.

[59] For differences in contents see Webster, *From Mycenae to Homer*, pp. 177–82, and for differences in style W. W. Minton, *TAPhA* 93 (1962), pp. 188–212.

[60] More evidence of contacts between the Mycenaeans and the Near East has become available since the discovery of Babylonian cylinder seals in the course of the new excavations at Thebes (E. Touloupa, *Kadmos* 3 (1964), pp. 25–7, and A. Falkenstein, ibid., pp. 108–9).

[61] Notopoulos, op. cit., p. 22.

[62] F. Schwenn, *Die Theogonie des Hesiodos* (Heidelberg, 1934), pp. 69–81.

SUPPLEMENTARY NOTE

Lambert's argument that the reign of Nebuchadnezzar I of Babylon is likely to have witnessed the composition of Enuma Elish (see our p. 37) appears to be gaining general acceptance. Thus in *Ancient Mesopotamia* (Chicago, 1964), the most recently published description of Mesopotamian civilization, Oppenheim remarks that Enuma Elish 'was written relatively late, though probably influenced by earlier texts and traditions' (p. 232), and later, when referring to a new outbreak of literary activity which produced the Epic of Era and texts associated with the Assyrian kings Tukulti-Ninurta I, Ashurnasirpal I, and Tiglath-pileser I and Nebuchadnezzar I of Babylon, says that 'it is quite possible that those phases of Mesopotamian literary history to which belong the poets or compilers of the Epic of Creation form part of this development' (pp. 268–9). Lambert himself discusses the claim of the reign of Nebuchadnezzar I to be considered a turning point in ancient Mesopotamian religion in *The Seed of Wisdom* (Toronto, 1964), pp. 3–13, and in *JThS* 16 (1965), pp. 287–300 takes a new look at the Babylonian background of Genesis. In the latter study Lambert comments that Enuma Elish 'is not a norm of Babylonian or Sumerian cosmology (see our p. 46). It is a sectarian and aberrant combination of mythological threads woven into an unparalleled compositum' (p. 291). After stating that he believes it to be not earlier than 1100 B.C., Lambert goes on to say that 'it happens to be the best preserved Babylonian document of its genre simply because it was at its height of popularity when the libraries were formed from which our knowledge of Babylonian mythology is mostly derived'. The history of Assyria and Babylonia between 1200 and 1000 B.C. is described by D. J. Wiseman, *Assyria and Babylonia, c. 1200–1000 B.C.* (*CAH*, fasc. 41, 1965).

P.W.

March 1966.

INDEX OF PASSAGES

I. HESIOD

II. HOMER

III. OTHER AUTHORS

GENERAL INDEX

11